CROWN FINANCIAL MINISTRIES

BIBLICAL

FINANCIAL

STUDY

SMALL GROUP STUDENT MANUAL

PO Box 100
Gainesville GA 30503-0100
1-800-722-1976 • www.crown.org

SMALL GROUP STUDY SCHEDULE

MY SMALL GROUP STUDY

Day and time it meets:_____ Date of first meeting:_____

Where it meets: _____

My leaders:_____ Phone: _____

_____ Phone: _____

NOTE: Any regularly scheduled class that falls on a holiday or other special event may be rescheduled.

WELCOME!

We are so thankful that you have decided to participate in the Crown small group study. The Lord has used the principles you are about to learn in the lives of hundreds of thousands of people who have taken the Crown study. We've learned that people benefit most when they are faithful to complete the following.

First of all, before the group meets, read *Your Money Counts*. This book is easy to read and will provide you with a good overview of the study. Then, complete these requirements before each weekly meeting.

1. HOMEWORK

- Complete the homework in writing. The homework questions are designed to take only about 15 minutes each day to complete. Space is provided in the Student Manual to answer the questions. If a married couple takes the study together, each will use a separate Student Manual.

2. SCRIPTURE MEMORY

- Memorize an assigned verse from the Bible each week and individually recite the verse at the beginning of class. This will help you remember the most important principles.

3. PRACTICAL APPLICATION

- Complete a practical financial exercise, such as beginning a budget or designing a debt repayment plan.

4. PRAYER

- Everyone prays for the other group members each day. Answers to prayers are one of the most encouraging parts of the small group experience.

If someone is unable to complete the requirements for a particular week, we've asked the leaders not to have him or her participate in the class discussion. This accountability helps us to be faithful. And the more faithful we are, the more benefits we receive from the study.

Attendance. Everyone should attend at least 8 of the 10 weekly meetings. Please notify one of the leaders in advance if you anticipate missing a meeting or arriving late. The meetings are designed to begin and end on time.

Again, we are very grateful you are going to participate in the Crown study. I pray that the Lord will bless you in every way as you learn His financial principles.

Howard Dayton

Howard Dayton, Author
CEO, Crown Financial Ministries

PURPOSE

*The purpose of the CROWN study
is to teach people God's financial principles
in order to know Christ more intimately
and to be free to serve Him.*

FINANCIAL POLICY

- CROWN FINANCIAL MINISTRIES does not endorse, recommend, or sell any financial investments. No one may use affiliation with CROWN to promote or influence the sale of any financial products or services.
- The CROWN FINANCIAL MINISTRIES small group study does not give specific investment advice. No one may use his or her affiliation with CROWN to give investment advice.
- This study is affordably priced because we do not want cost to be an obstacle to people who desire to participate. If you find the study valuable and want to help make it available to others, you may make a tax deductible gift to CROWN FINANCIAL MINISTRIES.

WEB SITE

CROWN has designed a Web site as a resource to provide students and leaders with up-to-date and detailed financial information. It contains helpful articles, a categorized list of the verses dealing with possessions, links to other useful Web sites, and much more.

Visit the Web site at **www.crown.org** for a world of information.

PERSONAL INFORMATION

A critical ingredient of taking part in a small group study is what happens after the study. It is our desire to provide important and useful resources and information that will assist you as you walk in the principles you are learning in this study. For us to do this we need to know who you are and how to get this information to you.

Please take a moment right now and fill out the Personal Information sheet found on page 5 of your *Practical Application Workbook*. After you have filled out this form, fold it, seal it, and drop it in the mail to us. No postage is necessary. Do not delay doing this. If you prefer, you may fill out the form online on our Web site, **www.crown.org**. To access this form type **www.crown.org/piform.asp**.

INTRODUCTION

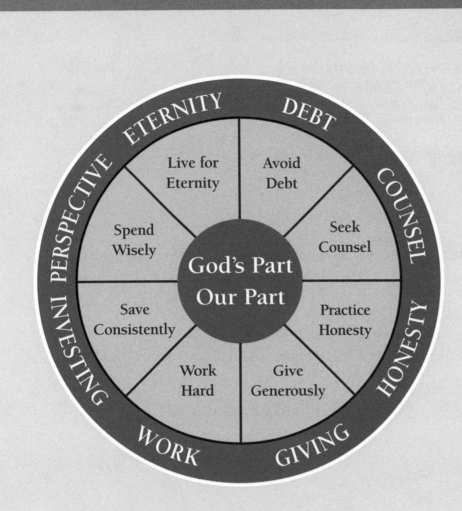

How We Handle Money Impacts Our Relationship with the Lord

"Therefore if you have not been faithful in the use of worldly wealth, who will entrust the true riches to you?"
(Luke 16:11).

INTRODUCTION HOMEWORK

To be completed for Week 1

Scripture to Memorize

"Therefore if you have not been faithful in the use of worldly* wealth, who will entrust the true riches to you?" (Luke 16:11).

* The word *worldly* from the *New International Version* has been substituted for the word *unrighteous* from the *New American Standard Bible* to clarify the meaning of this passage.

Before attending the first class, complete the ☐ Scripture to Memorize, ☐ Practical Application and ☐ Homework.

Practical Application: ☐ Read *Your Money Counts* prior to the first meeting.
☐ Fill out, fold, seal, and mail your Personal Information Sheet (or you may complete it online).

HOMEWORK

1. What was the most helpful information you learned from reading *Your Money Counts*?

Read *Isaiah 55:8-9*.

2. Based on this passage, do you think God's financial principles will differ from how most people handle money? What do you think would be the greatest difference?

INTRODUCTION

Read *Luke 16:11.*

3. What does this verse communicate to you about the importance of managing possessions faithfully?

4. How does handling money impact our fellowship with the Lord?

Scripture memory helps: The memory verses are found in the back of the *Practical Application Workbook* and are designed to be removed and carried with you throughout the day. The verses have been set to music on the CD located in the back of the *Practical Application Workbook*.

INTRODUCTION NOTES

Please do not read these notes until you have completed the Introduction Homework.

Jesus Christ said more about money than almost any other subject.

Two economic systems operate in the world: God's economy and economies that people invent. Scripture reveals God's economy to us in great detail.

The way most people handle money is in sharp contrast to God's financial principles. This should not surprise us. Isaiah 55:8 reads, *"'My thoughts are not your thoughts, nor are your ways My ways,' declares the Lord."* The most significant difference between these economic systems is that in God's economy, the living Lord plays the central role. As elementary as this sounds, this distinction has profound implications.

It is difficult for some people to think of God as being involved with our finances, because God has chosen to be invisible and operates in the unseen supernatural realm.

THE BIBLE AND MONEY

It may surprise you to learn just how much the Bible says about finances. There are more than 2,350 verses on how to handle money and possessions. And Jesus Christ said more about money than almost any other subject. Our Lord consistently addressed the issue of money for three reasons.

1. *How We Handle Our Money Influences Our Fellowship with the Lord*
Jesus equates how we handle our money with the quality of our spiritual life. In Luke 16:11, He says, *"Therefore if you have not been faithful in the use of worldly* wealth, who will entrust the true riches to you?"* If we handle our money properly according to the principles of Scripture, we grow closer to Christ. However, if we are unfaithful with it, our fellowship with Him will suffer.

This is illustrated in the parable of the talents. The master congratulates the servant who had managed money faithfully: *"Well done, good and faithful [servant]; you were faithful with a few things; I will put you in charge of many things. Enter into the joy of your master"* (Matthew 25:21). As we handle money God's way, we have an opportunity to enter into the joy of a more intimate relationship with our Lord. Sadly, this is a truth many people have failed to grasp.

2. *Possessions Compete with the Lord for First Place in our Lives*
Money is a primary competitor with Christ for the lordship of our lives. Jesus tells us we must choose to serve only one of these two masters. *"No one can*

* See note on page 8.

serve two masters. Either he will hate the one and love the other, or he will be devoted to the one and despise the other. You cannot serve both God and money" (Matthew 6:24, NIV). It is impossible for us to serve money—even in a small way—and still serve the Lord.

When the Crusades were being fought during the 12ᵗʰ Century, the Crusaders hired mercenaries to fight for them. Because it was a religious war, the mercenaries were baptized before fighting. As they were being baptized, the soldiers would take their swords and hold them out of the water to symbolize that Jesus Christ was not in control of their swords. They had the freedom to use their weapons in any way they wished.

Though they may not be as obvious about it as the soldiers were, many people today handle their money in a similar fashion. Some Christians hold their wallet or purse "out of the water," in effect saying, "God, you may be the lord of my entire life, except in the area of money—I am perfectly capable of handling that myself."

3. Much of Life Revolves Around the Use of Money

The Lord talked so much about money because He knew that much of our lives would center around its use. During your normal week, how much time do you spend earning money in your job, making decisions on how to spend money, thinking about where to save and invest money, or praying about your giving? Fortunately, God has prepared us by giving us the Bible as His roadmap for living.

> *God has certain responsibilities and has given other responsibilities to us. Most of the frustration we experience in handling money is because we do not realize which responsibilities are ours and which are not.*

A DIVISION OF RESPONSIBILITIES

A close friend, Jim Seneff, asked me to join him in a study of Scripture to find out what the Lord said about handling money. We read the entire Bible, identified each of the 2,350 verses, then arranged them by topics. Not only were we surprised at how practical the Word of God is in this area, but we discovered a division of responsibilities in the handling of our money. Simply put, God has a part, and we have a part.

God has certain responsibilities and has given other responsibilities to us. Most of the frustration we experience in handling money is because we do not realize which responsibilities are ours and which are not.

BEGIN THE JOURNEY

You will discover that learning and applying God's financial principles is a journey that takes time. When we learn God's responsibilities and do ours faithfully, we can experience contentment, hope, and confidence about our financial future. Let the journey begin!

GOD'S PART/OUR PART

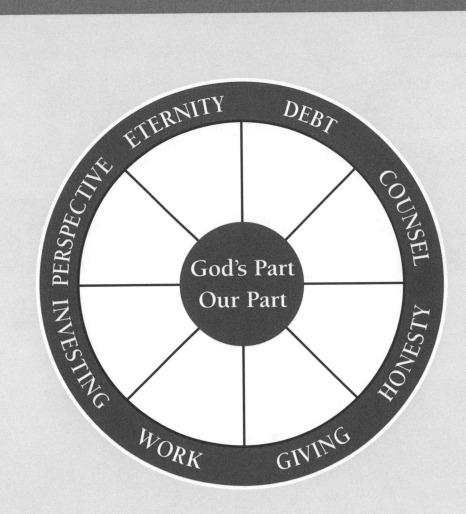

Lord Is Owner of All

"Everything in the heavens and earth is yours, O Lord"
(1 Chronicles 29:11, TLB).

Scripture to Memorize

"Everything in the heavens and earth is yours, O Lord, and this is your kingdom. We adore you as being in control of everything. Riches and honor come from you alone, and you are the Ruler of all mankind; your hand controls power and might, and it is at your discretion that men are made great and given strength" (1 Chronicles 29:11-12, TLB).

Practical Application

☐ Complete the Personal Financial Statement.   ☐ Begin recording everything you spend.
☐ Complete the Quit Claim Deed and bring it to be witnessed by members of your group.

DAY ONE

Read the Introduction Notes on pages 10 and 11 and answer.

1. What information especially interested you?

2. Comment on any personal challenges you felt after learning the three reasons the Bible says so much about money.

Read *Deuteronomy 10:14; Psalm 24:1;* and *1 Corinthians 10:26* and answer.

1. What do these passages teach about the ownership of your possessions?

Read *Leviticus 25:23; Psalm 50:10-12;* and *Haggai 2:8.*

2. What are some of the specific items that the Lord owns?

    Leviticus 25:23—

    Psalm 50:10-12—

    Haggai 2:8—

GOD'S PART/OUR PART

3. Prayerfully evaluate your attitude of ownership toward your possessions. Do you consistently recognize the true owner of those possessions? Give two practical suggestions to help recognize God's ownership.

■

■

Read *1 Chronicles 29:11-12* and *Psalm 135:6*.

1. What do these verses say about the Lord's control of circumstances?

Read *Proverbs 21:1*; *Isaiah 40:21-24*; and *Acts 17:26*.

2. What do these passages tell you about the Lord's control of people?

Proverbs 21:1—

Isaiah 40:21-24—

Acts 17:26—

3. Do you normally recognize the Lord's control of all events? If not, how can you become more consistent in recognizing His control?

DAY FOUR

Read *Genesis 45:4-8; Genesis 50:19-20; and Romans 8:28.*

1. Why is it important to realize that God controls and uses even difficult circumstances for good in the life a godly person?

2. How does this perspective impact you today?

3. Share a difficult circumstance you have experienced and how the Lord ultimately used it for good in your life.

Read *Psalm 34:9-10; Matthew 6:31-33;* and *Philippians 4:19.*

1. What has the Lord promised about meeting your needs?

2. From the Bible, give an example of the Lord providing for someone's needs in a supernatural way.

3. How does this apply to you today?

DAY SIX

Read *1 Corinthians 4:2.*

1. According to this verse what is your requirement as a steward?

2. How would you define a steward?

GOD'S PART/OUR PART

Read *Luke 16:1-2.*

3. Why did the master remove the steward from his position?

Read *Luke 16:10.*

4. Describe the principle found in this verse.

5. How does this apply in your situation?

 Please write your prayer requests in your Prayer Log before coming to class.

 I will take the following action as a result of this week's study.

GOD'S PART/OUR PART NOTES

Please do not read these notes until you have completed the God's Part/Our Part Homework.

In Scripture God calls Himself by more than 250 names. The name that best describes God's part in the area of money is Lord. This is the most important section of the entire study, because how we view God determines how we live.

After losing his children and all his possessions, Job was able to worship God because he knew His role as Lord of those possessions. Why did Moses forsake the treasures of Egypt and choose to suffer with the people of God? It was because Moses accepted God's role as Lord. There are three parts to God's position as Lord.

GOD'S PART

OWNERSHIP

The Lord owns all our possessions. *"To the Lord your God belong . . . the earth and everything in it"* (Deuteronomy 10:14, NIV). *"The earth is the Lord's, and all it contains"* (Psalm 24:1).

Scripture even reveals specific items God owns. Leviticus 25:23 identifies Him as the owner of all the land: *"The land . . . shall not be sold permanently, for the land is Mine."* Haggai 2:8 says that He owns the precious metals: *"'The silver is Mine and the gold is Mine,' declares the Lord of hosts."* And in Psalm 50 we are told God owns the animals.

> *"Every beast of the forest is Mine, the cattle on a thousand hills . . . everything that moves in the field is Mine. If I were hungry, I would not tell you, for the world is Mine, and all it contains"* (Psalm 50:10-12).

The Lord created all things, and He never transferred the ownership of His creation to people. In Colossians 1:17 we are told that, *"In Him all things hold together."* At this very moment the Lord holds everything together by His power. As we will see throughout this study, recognizing God's ownership is crucial in allowing Jesus Christ to become the Lord of our money and possessions.

Ownership or Lordship?

If we are going to be genuine followers of Christ, we must transfer ownership of our possessions to the Lord. *"None of you can be My disciple who does not give up all his own possessions"* (Luke 14:33). We must give up claim to own-

When we acknowledge God's ownership, every spending decision becomes a spiritual decision.

ership of all that we have. Sometimes the Lord will test us by asking us to be willing to give up the very possessions that are most important to us.

The most vivid example of this in Scripture is when the Lord instructed Abraham, *"Take now your son, your only son, whom you love, Isaac . . . and offer him there as a burnt offering"* (Genesis 22:2). When Abraham obeyed, demonstrating his willingness to give up his most valuable possession, God responded, *"Do not lay a hand on the boy . . . now I know that you fear God, because you have not withheld from Me your son"* (Genesis 22:12, NIV).

When we acknowledge God's ownership, every spending decision becomes a spiritual decision. No longer do we ask, "Lord, what do You want me to do with **my** money?" It becomes, "Lord, what do You want me to do with **Your** money?" When we have this attitude and handle His money according to His wishes, spending and saving decisions become as spiritual as giving decisions.

The Lord's ownership also influences how we care for possessions. For example, because the Lord is the owner of where we live we want to please Him by keeping His home or apartment cleaner and in better repair!

Recognizing God's Ownership

Consistently recognizing God's ownership can be difficult. It is easy to believe intellectually that God owns all you have but still live as if this were not true. Our culture suggests an opposing view. Everything around us—the media, even the law—says that what you possess you own. Genuinely acknowledging God's ownership requires nothing less than a new way of thinking.

Here are a number of practical suggestions to help us recognize God's ownership.

- For the next 30 days meditate on 1 Chronicles 29:11-12 when you first awake and just before going to sleep.
- Be careful in the use of personal pronouns; consider substituting "the" or "the Lord's" for "my," "mine," and "ours."
- Ask the Lord to make you aware of His ownership and make you willing to give up ownership. Pray for this during the next 30 days.
- Establish the habit of acknowledging the Lord's ownership every time you purchase an item.

Recognizing the Lord's ownership is important in learning contentment. If you believe that you own a particular possession, then the circumstances surrounding that possession will affect your attitude. If it's a favorable situation, you will be happy. If it's a difficult circumstance, you will be discontent.

Shortly after Jim came to grips with God's ownership, he purchased a car. He had driven the car only two days before someone rammed into the side of it. Jim's first reaction was "Lord, I don't know why You want a dent in Your car, but now You've got a big one!" Jim was learning contentment!

If you believe that you own a particular possession, then the circumstances surrounding that possession will affect your attitude. If it's a favorable situation, you will be happy. If it's a difficult circumstance, you will be discontent.

CONTROL

Besides being Creator and Owner, God is ultimately in control of every event that occurs upon the earth. *"We adore you as being in control of everything"* (1 Chronicles 29:11, TLB). *"Whatever the Lord pleases, He does, in heaven and in earth"* (Psalm 135:6). And in the book of Daniel, King Nebuchadnezzar stated: *"I praised the Most High; I honored and glorified Him who lives forever. . . . All the peoples of the earth are regarded as nothing. He does as He pleases with the powers of heaven and the peoples of the earth. No one can hold back His hand or say to him: 'What have you done?'"* (Daniel 4:34-35, NIV).

The Lord is in control even of difficult events. *"I am the Lord, and there is no other, the One forming light and creating darkness, causing well-being and creating calamity; I am the Lord who does all these"* (Isaiah 45:6-7).

It is important for us to realize that our heavenly Father uses even seemingly devastating circumstances for ultimate good in the lives of the godly. *"We know that God causes all things to work together for good to those who love God, to those who are called according to His purpose"* (Romans 8:28). The Lord allows difficult circumstances for three reasons.

1. He Accomplishes His Intentions

This is illustrated in the life of Joseph who, as a teenager, was sold into slavery by his jealous brothers. Joseph understood this later and responded to his brothers: *"Do not be distressed and do not be angry with yourselves for selling me here, because it was to save lives that God sent me ahead of you. . . . It was not you who sent me here, but God. . . . You intended to harm me, but God intended it for good to accomplish what is now being done, the saving of many lives"* (Genesis 45:5, 8; 50:20, NIV).

2. He Develops Our Character

Godly character, something that is precious in the sight of the Lord, often is developed during trying times.

> *"We also rejoice in our sufferings, because we know that suffering produces perseverance; perseverance, character"* (Romans 5:3-4, NIV).

3. He Disciplines His Children

> *"Those whom the Lord loves He disciplines. . . . He disciplines us for our good, so that we may share His holiness. All discipline for the moment seems not to be joyful, but sorrowful; yet to those who have been trained by it, afterwards it yields the peaceful fruit of righteousness"* (Hebrews 12:6,10-11).

When we are disobedient, we can expect our loving Lord to discipline us, often through difficult circumstances, to encourage us to abandon our sin and "share His holiness."

You can be at peace knowing that your loving heavenly Father is in control of every situation that you will ever face, and He intends to use every one for a good purpose.

Godly character, something that is precious in the sight of the Lord, often is developed during trying times.

GOD IS THE PROVIDER

The Lord promises to provide our needs. *"Seek first His kingdom and His righteousness, and all these things* [food and clothing] *shall be given to you"* (Matthew 6:33, NIV).

The same Lord who fed manna to the children of Israel during their 40 years of wandering in the wilderness and who fed 5,000 with only five loaves and two fish has promised to provide our needs. This is the same Lord who told Elijah, *"I have commanded the ravens to provide for you. . . . The ravens brought him bread and meat in the morning and bread and meat in the evening"* (1 Kings 17:4,6).

God is both predictable and unpredictable. He is totally predictable in His faithfulness to provide for our needs. What we cannot predict is *how* the Lord will provide. He uses various and often surprising means—an increase in income or a gift. He may provide an opportunity to stretch limited resources through money-saving purchases. Regardless of how He chooses to provide for our needs, He is completely reliable.

The Lord instructs us to be content when our basic needs are met. *"If we have food and clothing, we will be content"* (1 Timothy 6:8, NIV). Charles Allen tells a story that illustrates this principle. As World War II was drawing to a close, the Allied armies gathered up many orphans and placed them in camps where they were well fed. Despite excellent care, they were afraid and slept poorly.

Finally, a doctor came up with a solution. The children each were given a piece of bread to hold after they were put to bed. If they were hungry, more food was provided; but, after they finished, this particular piece of bread was just to be held—not eaten. The piece of bread produced wonderful results. The children went to bed knowing that they would have food to eat the next day. That guarantee gave the children restful sleep.

Similarly, the Lord has given us His guarantee—our "piece of bread." As we cling to His promises of provision, we can relax and be content. *"My God shall supply all your needs according to His riches"* (Philippians 4:19).

Needs Versus Wants

It is important to understand the difference between a need and a want. The definition of a need is one of the **basic necessities of life**, which are food, clothing, and shelter. A want is **anything in excess of a need**. The Lord may allow us to have our wants fulfilled, but He has not promised to provide *all* of them.

God, as He is revealed in Scripture, is much different than the way most people imagine Him to be.

GETTING TO KNOW GOD

God, as He is revealed in Scripture, is much different than the way most people imagine Him to be. Our tendency is to shrink God down and fit Him into a mold with human abilities and limitations. We do not understand the greatness of God, *"who stretched out the heavens and laid the foundations of the earth"* (Isaiah 51:13). We expand our perspective of God primarily through studying what the Bible tells us about Him. The following are a few samples.

He Is Lord of the Universe

Carefully review some of His names and attributes: Creator, the Almighty, eternal, all-knowing, all-powerful, awesome, Lord of lords and King of kings.

The Lord's power and ability are beyond our understanding. Astronomers estimate that there are more than 100 billion galaxies in the universe, each containing billions of stars. The distance from one end of a galaxy to the other is often measured in millions of light years. Though our sun is a relatively small star, it could contain more than one million earths, and it has temperatures of 20 million degrees at its center. Isaiah wrote,

> *"Lift up your eyes on high and see who has created these stars, the One who leads forth their host by number, He calls them all by name; because of the greatness of His might and the strength of His power, not one of them is missing"* (Isaiah 40:26).

He Is Lord of the Nations

Examine how much greater the Lord is compared to nations and people. Isaiah 40:21-24 tells us, *"Do you not know? Have you not heard? . . . It is He who sits above the circle of the earth, and its inhabitants are like grasshoppers . . . He it is who reduces rulers to nothing, who makes the judges of the earth meaningless. Scarcely have they been planted, scarcely have they been sown, scarcely has their stock taken root in the earth, but He merely blows on them, and they wither."*

From Isaiah 40:15, 17 we read, *"The nations are like a drop from a bucket, and are regarded as a speck of dust on the scales. . . . All the nations are as nothing before Him, they are regarded by Him as less than nothing and meaningless."*

God doesn't fret over nations and their leaders as if He had no power to intervene. Acts 17:26 says, *"He [the Lord] . . . scattered the nations across the face of the earth. He decided beforehand which should rise and fall, and when. He determined their boundaries"* (TLB).

He Is Lord of the Individual

God is intimately involved with each of us as individuals. Psalm 139:3-4, 16 reveals, *"You are familiar with all my ways. Before a word is on my tongue you know it completely, O Lord. . . . All the days ordained for me were written in your book before one of them came to be"* (NIV). The Lord is so involved in our lives that He reassures us, *"The very hairs of your head are all numbered"* (Matthew 10:30). Our heavenly Father is the One who knows us the best and loves us the most.

God hung the stars in space, fashioned the earth's towering mountains and mighty oceans, and determined the destiny of nations. Jeremiah observed: *"Nothing is too difficult for You"* (Jeremiah 32:17). Yet God knows when a sparrow falls to the ground. Nothing in this study is more important than "catching the vision" of who God is and what His part is in our finances.

God hung the stars in space, fashioned the earth's towering mountains and mightly oceans, and determined the destiny of nations. Jeremiah observed: "Nothing is too difficult for You" (Jeremiah 32:17). Yet God knows when a sparrow falls to the ground.

The Lord did not design people to shoulder the responsibilities that only He can carry. Jesus said, *"Come to Me, all who are weary and heavy-laden, and I will give you rest. Take My yoke upon you. . . . For My yoke is easy, and My burden is light"* (Matthew 11:28-30). God has assumed the burdens of ownership, control, and provision. For this reason, His yoke is easy and we can rest and enjoy the peace of God.

For most of us, the problem is that we do not always recognize God's part. Our culture contributes to this problem. God is thought to play no part in financial matters, and we have, in some measure, been influenced by that view. Another reason for this difficulty is that God has chosen to be invisible. Anything that is "out of sight" tends to become "out of mind." We get out of the habit of recognizing His ownership, control, and provision.

After learning God's Part, some think that little responsibility remains for us. However, the Lord has given us great responsibility.

OUR PART

The word that best describes our part is steward. A steward is a manager of someone else's possessions. The Lord has given us the authority to be stewards. *"You made him ruler over the works of your* [the Lord's] *hands; you put everything under his feet"* (Psalm 8:6, NIV).

Our responsibility is summed up in this verse: *"It is required of stewards that one be found trustworthy"* (1 Corinthians 4:2). Before we can be faithful, we must know what we are required to do. Just as the purchaser of a complicated piece of machinery studies the manufacturer's manual to learn how to operate it, we need to examine the Creator's handbook—the Bible—to determine how He wants us to handle His possessions.

As we begin to study our responsibilities, it's important to remember that God loves and cares for us deeply. He has given us these principles because He wants the best for us. Most people discover areas in which they have not been faithful. Don't be come discouraged. Simply seek to apply faithfully what you learn.

Now, there are two elements of our responsibility that are important to understand.

1. Be Faithful with What We Are Given
We are to be faithful regardless of how much He has entrusted to us. The parable of the talents (a talent was a sum of money) illustrates this.

> *"It will be like a man going on a journey, who called his servants and entrusted his property to them. To one he gave five talents of money, to another two talents, and to another one talent"* (Matthew 25:14-15, NIV).

Our responsibility is summed up in this verse: "It is required of stewards that one be found trustworthy" (1 Corinthians 4:2).

When the owner returned, he held each one responsible for faithfully managing his possessions. The owner praised the faithful servant who received the five talents: *"Well done, good and faithful* [servant]. *You were faithful with a few things, I will put you in charge of many things; enter into the* joy *of your master"* (Matthew 25:21). Interestingly, the servant who had been given two talents received the identical reward as the one who had been given the five talents (see Matthew 25:23). The Lord rewards faithfulness, regardless of the amount over which we are responsible.

We are required to be faithful whether we are given much or little. As someone once said, "It's not what I would do if $1 million were my lot; it's what I am doing with the $10 I've got."

2. Be Faithful in Every Area
God wants us to be faithful in handling all of our money. Unfortunately, most Christians have been taught only how to handle 10 percent of their income God's way—the area of giving. And although this area is crucial, most have learned how to handle the other 90 percent from the world's perspective.

Study this diagram.

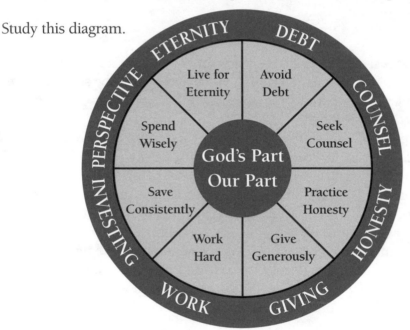

As a result of not being taught to handle money biblically, many Christians have wrong attitudes toward possessions. This often causes them to make incorrect financial decisions and to suffer painful consequences. Hosea 4:6 reads, *"My people are destroyed for lack of knowledge."*

BENEFITS OF HANDLING MONEY FAITHFULLY

The faithful steward enjoys three benefits.

1. More Intimate Fellowship with Jesus Christ
Remember what the master said to the servant who had been faithful with his

finances: *"Enter into the joy of your master"* (Matthew 25:21). We can enter into closer, more intimate fellowship with our Lord when we are faithful with the possessions He has given us.

Someone once told me that the Lord often allows a person to teach a subject because the teacher desperately needs it! That is true for me in the area of money. I have never met anyone who had more wrong attitudes about money or who handled money in a way more contrary to Scripture than I did. When I began to apply these principles, I experienced a dramatic improvement in my fellowship with the Lord. Each of these principles is intended to draw us closer to Christ.

2. The Development of Character

God uses money to refine character. As David McConaugh explained in his book, *Money the Acid Test* (written in 1918), "Money, most common of temporal things, involves uncommon and eternal consequences. Even though it may be done quite unconsciously, money molds people in the process of getting it, saving it, spending it, and giving it. Depending on how it's used, it proves to be a blessing or a curse. Either the person becomes master of the money, or the money becomes the master of the person. Our Lord uses money to test our lives and as an instrument to mold us into the likeness of Himself."

All through Scripture there is a correlation between the development of a person's character and how he or she handles money. It is regarded as an index to a person's true character. You have heard the expression, "Money talks," and indeed it does. You can tell a lot about a person's character by examining his or her checkbook and credit card statement, because we spend our money on the things that are most important to us.

3. Having Our Finances in Order

As we apply God's principles to our finances, we will begin to get out of debt, spend more wisely, start saving for our future, and give even more to the work of Christ.

PRINCIPLES OF FAITHFULNESS

1. If We Waste Possessions, the Lord Will Remove Us As Stewards.

> *"There was a certain rich man who had a manager [steward], and this [steward] was reported to him as squandering his possessions. And he called him and said to him, 'What is this I hear about you? Give an account of your management [stewardship], for you can no longer be [steward]'"* (Luke 16:1-2).

Two principles from this passage are applicable to us. First of all, when we waste our possessions it becomes public knowledge and creates a poor testimony. *"This [steward] was reported to him as squandering his possessions."* Secondly, the Lord may remove us as stewards if we squander what He has given us.

A businessman earned a fortune in just three years and then went on a spending spree. Two years later he informed his office staff that he had little left and everyone would need to economize. Shortly thereafter, he left for an expensive vacation and had his office completely renovated at a cost of thousands of dollars.

During his vacation the entire staff gathered in the newly decorated office to discuss his unbridled spending habits. The Lord soon removed this man from the privilege of being steward over much, and today he is on the verge of bankruptcy.

This principle is applicable today. If you waste the possessions entrusted to you, you may not be given more.

2. Faithfulness in Little Things

> "He who is faithful in a very little thing is faithful also in much; and he who is unrighteous in a very little thing is unrighteous also in much" (Luke 16:10).

How do you know if your son is going to take good care of his first car? Observe how he cared for his bicycle. How do you know if a salesperson will do a competent job of serving a large client? Evaluate how he or she serves a small client. If we have the character to be faithful with small things, the Lord knows He can trust us with greater responsibilities. Small things are small things, but faithfulness with a small thing is a big thing.

3. Faithfulness with Another's Possessions

In some measure, faithfulness with another's possession will determine how much you are given. *"If you have not been faithful in the use of that which is another's, who will give you that which is your own?"* (Luke 16:12).

This is a principle that is often overlooked. One of the most faithful men I know rented a vehicle from a friend. While driving the vehicle, he was involved in an accident. After explaining the situation to the owner, he took the vehicle to the owner's mechanic and instructed him, "Completely restore this vehicle. Make it better than it was before the accident, and I will be responsible for the bill." What an example!

Are you faithful with others' possessions? Are you careless with your employer's office supplies? Do you waste electricity when you are staying in a hotel room? When someone allows you to use something, are you careful to return it promptly and in good shape? Some people have not been entrusted with more because they have been unfaithful with the possessions of others.

Please prayerfully review these principles of faithfulness.

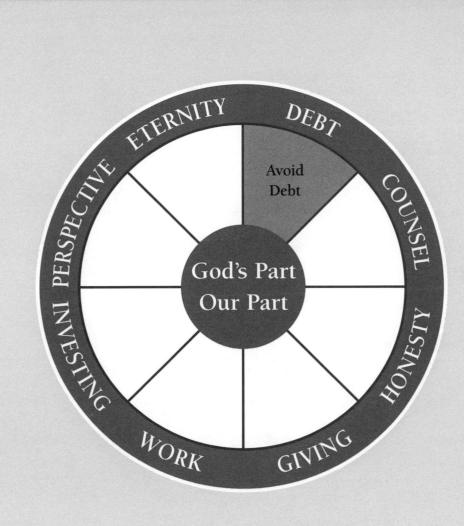

Debt Is Slavery

"Just as the rich rule the poor, so the borrower is servant to the lender"

(Proverbs 22:7, TLB).

DEBT HOMEWORK 👑

To Be Completed for Week 3

 Scripture to Memorize

"Just as the rich rule the poor, so the borrower is servant to the lender" (Proverbs 22:7, TLB).

Practical Application: ☐ Complete the Debt List and the ☐ Debt Repayment Schedule for each creditor.

DAY ONE

Read the God's Part/Our Part Notes on pages 20 to 28.

1. How have you observed the Lord using money to mold your character?

2. What strengths have been developed in your character?

3. What weaknesses in your character still need to be addressed?

DEBT

Read *Deuteronomy 15:4-6; Deuteronomy 28:1, 2, 12; and Deuteronomy 28:15, 43-45.*

1. According to these passages how was debt viewed in the Old Testament?

2. What was the cause of someone getting in debt (becoming a borrower) or getting out of debt (becoming a lender)?

DAY THREE

Read *Romans 13:8; Proverbs 22:7; and 1 Corinthians 7:23.*

1. Is debt encouraged in Scripture? Why?

   Romans 13:8 —

   Proverbs 22:7 —

   1 Corinthians 7:23 —

2. How does this apply to you personally and to your business?

3. If you are in debt, do you have a strategy to get out of debt? If you have a plan, please describe it.

Read *Psalm 37:21* **and** *Proverbs 3:27-28.*

1. What do these verses say about debt repayment?

 Psalm 37:21—

 Proverbs 3:27-28—

2. How will you implement this?

Read *2 Kings 4:1-7.*

1. What principles of getting out of debt can you identify from this passage?

2. Can you apply any of these principles to your present situation? How?

DAY SIX

Read *Proverbs 22:26-27 and Proverbs 17:18.*

1. What does the Bible say about cosigning (striking hands, surety)?

    Proverbs 22:26-27—

    Proverbs 17:18—

Read *Proverbs 6:1-5.*

2. If someone has cosigned, what should he or she attempt to do?

 Please write your prayer requests in your Prayer Log before coming to class.

 I will take the following action as a result of this week's study.

DEBT NOTES

Please do not read these notes until you have completed the Debt Homework.

"TILL DEBT DO US PART"

The amount of debt in our nation has exploded—government debt, business debt, and personal debt. Individuals owe more than $7 trillion. The average household spends $400 more than it earns each year. Personal consumer debt increases at the rate of $1,000 a second!

We have so much personal debt in our country that the average person has been described as someone driving on a bond-financed highway, in a bank-financed car, fueled by charge card-financed gasoline, going to purchase furniture on an installment plan to put in a savings-and-loan-financed home!

We are drowning in a sea of debt. And, with all this credit floating around, we have serious financial casualties. In a recent year more than 1,300,000 individuals filed bankruptcy. And most sobering, a Gallup Poll found that 56 percent of all divorces are a result of financial tension in the home.

Such financial tension is created largely by believing the "Gospel According to Madison Avenue": buy now and pay later with easy monthly payments. We all know that nothing about those monthly payments is easy. Advertisers fail to tell us the whole truth. They leave out one little word: *debt*.

WHAT IS DEBT?

The dictionary defines debt as "money that a person is obligated to pay to another." Debt includes money owed to credit card companies, bank loans, money borrowed from relatives, the home mortgage, and past due medical bills. Bills that come due, such as the monthly electrical bill, are not considered debt if they are paid on time.

We need to understand the real cost of debt. Assume you have $5,560 in credit card debt at an 18 percent interest rate. This would cost you $1,000 in interest annually. Study the chart below.

1. Amount of interest you paid

Year 5	Year 10	Year 20	Year 30	Year 40
$5,000	$10,000	$20,000	$30,000	$40,000

2. What you would accumulate on $1,000 invested annually earning 12 percent

Year 5	Year 10	Year 20	Year 30	Year 40
6,353	17,549	72,052	241,333	767,091

3. How much the lender earns from your interest payment at 18 percent interest

Year 5	Year 10	Year 20	Year 30	Year 40
7,154	23,521	146,628	790,948	4,163,213

You can see what lenders have known for a long time: the incredible impact of compounding interest working for them. The lender will accumulate more than $4 million if you pay $1,000 a year for 40 years, and the lender earns 18 percent on your payment! Is there any wonder credit card companies are eager for you to become one of their borrowers?

Now compare the $40,000 you paid in interest over 40 years with the $767,091 you could have accumulated, earning 12 percent on $1,000 each year. The monthly income on $767,091 is $7,671 if it's earning 12 percent—without ever touching the principal.

Stop to consider this: When a you assume debt of $5,560 and pay $1,000 a year in interest, if a 12 percent return is earned on an investment, it actually costs you $767,091 over 40 years. Debt has a much higher cost than many realize. Next time you are tempted to purchase something with debt, ask yourself if the long-term benefits of staying out of debt outweigh the short-term benefits of the purchase.

Home Mortgage

A 30-year home mortgage, at a 10 percent interest rate, will require you to pay more than **three times** the amount originally borrowed.

Original mortgage amount	$100,000.00
Monthly mortgage payment at 10 percent interest	$877.57
Months paid	x 360
Total payments	**$315,925.20**

The Physical Cost of Debt

Debt also often increases stress, which contributes to mental, physical, and emotional fatigue. It can stifle creativity and harm relationships. Many people raise their lifestyle through debt, only to discover that the burden of debt then controls their lifestyle. The car bumper sticker that reads, "I owe, I owe, it's off to work I go," is an unfortunate reality for too many people.

"I see your problem. You've got your creditors on your back."

WHAT SCRIPTURE SAYS ABOUT DEBT

Scripture does not say that debt is a sin, but it discourages the use of debt. Remember, God loves us and has given us these principles for our benefit. Read the first portion of Romans 13:8 carefully from several different Bible translations: *"Owe no man any thing"* (KJV). *"Let no debt remain outstanding"* (NIV). *"Pay all your debts"* (TLB). *"Owe nothing to anyone"* (NASB). *"Keep out of debt and owe no man anything"* (Amplified).

1. Debt Is Considered Slavery

Proverbs 22:7 reads: *"Just as the rich rule the poor, so the borrower is servant to the lender"* (TLB). When we are in debt, we are in a position of servitude to the lender. And the deeper we are in debt, the more like servants we become. We do not have the freedom to decide where to spend our income, because our money is already obligated to meet these debts.

In 1 Corinthians 7:23 Paul writes, *"You were bought with a price; do not become slaves of men."* Our Father made the ultimate sacrifice by giving His Son, the Lord Jesus Christ, to die for us. And He now wants His children free to serve Him, not lenders, in whatever way He chooses.

2. Debt Was Considered a Curse

In the Old Testament, being out of debt was one of the promised rewards for obedience.

> *"If you diligently obey the Lord your God, being careful to do all His commandments which I command you today, the Lord your God will set you high above all the nations of the earth. All these blessings will come upon you. . . . You shall lend to many nations, but you shall not borrow"* (Deuteronomy 28:1, 2, 12).

However, debt was one of the curses for disobedience. *"If you do not obey the Lord your God, to observe to do all His commandments and His statutes with which I charge you today, that all these curses will come upon you and overtake you. . . . The alien who is among you shall rise above you higher and higher, but you will go down lower and lower. He shall lend to you, but you will not lend to him; he shall be the head, and you will be the tail"* (Deuteronomy 28:15,43,44).

3. Debt Presumes Upon Tomorrow

When we get into debt, we assume that we will earn enough in the future to pay the debt. We plan for our jobs to continue or our businesses or investments to be profitable. Scripture cautions us against presumption: *"Come now, you who say, 'Today or tomorrow, we shall go to such and such a city, and spend a year there and engage in business and make a profit.' Yet you do not know what your life will be like tomorrow. You are just a vapor that appears for a little while and then vanishes away. Instead, you ought to say, 'If the Lord wills, we shall live and also do this or that'"* (James 4:13-15).

4. Debt May Deny God an Opportunity

Ron Blue, an outstanding financial author, tells of a young man who wanted to go to seminary to become a missionary. The young man had no money and thought the only way he could afford seminary was to secure a student loan. However, this would have left him with $40,000 of debt by the time he graduated, which would have been impossible to pay back on a missionary's salary.

After a great deal of prayer, he decided to enroll without the help of a student loan and to trust the Lord to meet his needs. He graduated without borrowing anything and grew in his appreciation for how God could creatively provide his needs. This was the most valuable lesson learned in seminary as he prepared for life on the mission field. Borrowing may deny God an opportunity to demonstrate His reality.

BORROWING

Scripture is silent on the subject of when we can owe money. In our opinion it is possible to owe money for a home mortgage or for your business or vocation. This is permissible, we believe, only if the following three criteria are met.

- The item purchased is an asset with the potential to appreciate or produce an income.
- The value of an item equals or exceeds the amount owed against it.
- The debt should not be so high that repayment puts undue strain on the budget.

Here's how a home mortgage might qualify. Usually, the home has been an appreciating asset, so it meets the first requirement. If you invest a reasonable down payment, you could expect to sell the home for at least enough to pay off the mortgage, and this meets the second requirement. Lastly, the monthly house payment should not strain your budget.

If you meet the criteria and assume some "debt," we pray you will immediately establish the goal of eliminating even this debt. There is no assurance that the housing market will appreciate. A loss of job can interrupt your income. Please consider paying off all debt.

HOW TO GET OUT OF DEBT

There are ten steps for getting out of debt. The steps are easy, but following them requires *hard work*. The goal is D-Day—Debtless Day when you become absolutely free of debt.

1. Pray

In 2 Kings 4:1-7 we read about a widow who was threatened with losing her children to her creditor, and she asked Elisha for help. Elisha instructed the widow to borrow many empty jars from her neighbors. The Lord multiplied her only possession—a small amount of oil—and all the jars were filled. She sold the oil and paid her debts to free her children.

The same God who provided supernaturally for the widow is interested in you becoming free from debt. The first step is to pray. Seek the Lord's help and guidance in your journey toward Debtless Day. He may act immediately, as in the case of the widow, or slowly over time. In either case, prayer is essential.

A trend is emerging. As people begin to eliminate debt, the Lord has blessed their faithfulness. Even if you can afford only a small monthly prepayment of your debt, please do it. The Lord can multiply your efforts.

2. Establish a Budget

In our experience, few people in debt have been using a budget. They may have had one—neatly filed away in a drawer or loaded on their computer—but they have not been using it. A budget helps you plan ahead and control the biggest budget buster of them all: impulse spending.

3. List Everything You Own

Evaluate your possessions to determine if there is anything you do not need that might be sold to help you to get out of debt more quickly. What about the clothes you no longer wear? That set of golf clubs gathering dust? Is there anything you can sell to help you to get out of debt?

4. List Everything You Owe

Many people, particularly if they owe a lot of money, do not know exactly what they owe. It must be human nature: If we avoid unpleasant things, perhaps they will go away. However, you need to list your debts to determine your current financial situation.

5. Establish a Debt Repayment

Part of the practical application this week is establishing a repayment schedule for each debt. We suggest you decide which debts to pay off first based on two factors.

- *Pay off small debts first.* Focus on paying off smaller debts first. You will be encouraged as they are eliminated, and this will free up cash to apply against other debts. After you pay off the first debt, apply its payment toward the next debt you wish to retire. After the second debt is paid off, apply what you were paying on the first and second debts toward the next debt you wish to eliminate, and so forth.
- *Pay off higher interest rate debts.* Determine what rate of interest you are being charged on each debt, and try to pay off first those that charge the highest rate of interest.

Ziggy/Tom Wilson. Used by permission. United Press Syndicate.

6. Consider Earning Additional Income

Many people hold jobs that simply do not pay enough to meet their needs, even if they spend wisely. If you earn additional income, decide in advance to pay off debts with the added earnings. We tend to spend more than we make, whether we earn much or little, so be careful of falling into the trap of spending the extra income.

7. Control the Use of Credit Cards

A wave of credit card solicitations is overwhelming our mailboxes. Many of these are deceptive, promising low interest rates, which rise to high levels within a few months. Credit cards are not sinful, but they are dangerous. It is estimated that people carry more than one billion credit cards, and only 40 percent of them are paid in full each month. People spend about one-third more when they use credit cards rather than cash, because they feel they are not really spending money (because it's just plastic). As one shopper said to another, "I like credit cards lots more than money, because they go so much further!"

When we examine the finances of someone in debt, we use a simple rule of thumb to determine whether credit cards are too dangerous for them. If they do not pay the entire balance at the end of each month, we encourage them to perform some plastic surgery—any good scissors will do.

8. Be Content with What You Have

The advertising industry uses powerful methods to get consumers to buy. Frequently the message is intended to create discontentment with what we have. An example is the American company that opened a new plant in Central America because the labor was relatively inexpensive. Everything went well until the villagers received their first paycheck; afterward they did not return to work. Several days later, the manager went down to the village chief to determine the cause of this problem, and the chief responded, "Why should we work? We already have everything we need." The plant stood idle for two months until someone came up with the idea of sending a mail-order catalog to every villager. There has not been an employment problem since!

Note these three realities of our consumer-driven economy.

- The more television you watch, the more you spend.
- The more you look at catalogs and magazines, the more you spend.
- The more you shop, the more you spend.

Our family has been living proof of this. I could tell when my six-year-old daughter had been watching television, because suddenly she had to have a special glass from a fast-food restaurant. Limiting our television viewing also limits our wants.

There is an interesting passage in 1 Timothy 6:5-6: " . . . *men of depraved mind and deprived of the truth . . . suppose that godliness is a means of gain. But godliness actually is a means of great gain when accompanied by contentment.*" I puzzled over this passage until I met a man who had recently come to know Christ. He told me that before he was introduced to Christ he would take his friends to the most expensive restaurants in town. But now that he is growing in his relationship with the Lord he spends less. Because he is not trying to impress everyone, he can meet his friends at far less expensive places and concentrate on developing healthy relationships. Being content in Christ is a means of great gain.

9. Consider a Radical Change in Lifestyle

A growing number of people have lowered their standard of living significantly to get out of debt more quickly. Some have sold a home and moved to a smaller one or rented an apartment or moved in with family members. Many have sold automobiles with large monthly payments and have purchased inexpensive used cars for cash. In short, they have temporarily sacrificed their standard of living to be free from debt in a shorter period of time.

10. Do Not Give Up!

The last step is most difficult in getting out of debt. On October 29, 1941, Winston Churchill, Prime Minister of England, was invited to give a school commencement address. At the time, World War II was overwhelming all of Europe, and England's fate was in doubt. Churchill stood to speak and said, "Never give in. Never give in. Never, never, never—in nothing, great or small large or petty—never give in except to convictions of honor and good sense." Then he sat down.

Never give up in your efforts to get out of debt. It may require hard work and sacrifice, but the freedom is worth the struggle.

If you need a professional debt manager to help you negotiate with creditors or establish a debt repayment plan, we recommend Financial Hope at **www.financialhope.com.**

ESCAPING THE AUTO-DEBT TRAP

Automobile loans are one of the leading causes of consumer indebtedness. Seventy percent of all the automobiles are financed. Here's how to escape this trap. First of all, decide in advance to keep your car for at least three years longer that your existing car debt. Second, pay off your automobile loan. Third, continue paying the monthly car payment, but pay it into a special account for your next car. Then, when you are ready to replace your car, the saved cash plus the trade-in should be sufficient to buy your car without credit. It may not be a new car, but you should be able to purchase a reliable used car, without any debt.

THE HOME MORTGAGE

If you own a home or plan to purchase one in the future, we want to encourage you to pay it off more rapidly than scheduled.

When my wife Bev and I first learned God's financial principles, we decided to work toward paying off everything, including the home mortgage. Frankly, this was an unrealistic goal for us at the time, but we began to explore how we might do it.

Let's examine the payment schedule for a home mortgage. Please do not let the size of the mortgage or the rate of interest hinder your thinking; this is for illustration purposes only. In the chart below, we are assuming a $100,000 mortgage at a 10 percent interest rate, paid over 30 years. The first year of the payment schedule would look like this.

PAYMENT # / MONTH		PAYMENT	INTEREST	PRINCIPAL	PRINCIPAL BALANCE
1	Jan	877.57	833.33	44.24	99,955.76
2	Feb	877.57	832.96	44.61	99,911.15
3	Mar	877.57	832.59	44.98	99,866.17
4	Apr	877.57	832.22	45.35	99,820.82
5	May	877.57	831.84	45.73	99,775.09
6	Jun	877.57	831.46	46.11	99,728.98
7	Jul	877.57	831.07	46.50	99,682.48
8	Aug	877.57	830.69	46.88	99,635.60
9	Sep	877.57	830.30	47.27	99,588.33
10	Oct	877.57	829.90	47.67	99,540.66
11	Nov	877.57	829.51	48.06	99,492.60
12	Dec	877.57	829.10	48.47	99,444.13
TOTALS FOR YEAR:		10,530.84	9,974.97	555.87	

"Godliness actually is a means of great gain when accompanied by contentment" (*1 Timothy 6:6*).

D E B T   N O T E S

As you can see, the payments during the early years are almost all interest. Of the $10,530 in payments made this first year, only $555 went toward principal reduction! In fact, it will be 23½ years before the principal and the interest portions of the payment equal each other! I don't know about you, but a 30-year goal to pay off a home mortgage is just too long. If this can be reduced to 15 years, then the goal becomes much more attainable. There are several methods we can use to pay off the mortgage in half the time.

One method is to increase the amount of your monthly payment by a regular amount. In our example, a $100,000 mortgage at 10 percent interest payable over 30 years requires a monthly installment of $877. If you increase the monthly payment by $197 to pay $1,074, the mortgage will be paid in 15 years. During the 15 years you will have made $35,467 in advance payments on the principal. This will have saved you $122,495 in interest over the life of your mortgage.

A second method is to prepay the next month's principal payment in addition to your regular monthly payment of $877. By doing this consistently for 15 years you will have paid off the entire mortgage. During the early years, the additional payment is low, but in the later years the extra payment will become much larger.

Study your mortgage to confirm that the mortgage may be prepaid without any penalty. A home mortgage usually allows such prepayment. And, finally, let your lender know what you are planning

There are three primary arguments against this. (1) Why pay off a low-interest home mortgage when you can earn more elsewhere? (2) With inflation, the lender is being paid back with less valuable dollars during the life of the mortgage. (3) You are losing a tax shelter because the interest paid on a home mortgage is a tax deduction.

Rather than addressing these arguments directly, we should recognize that the tax system in America is designed to reward indebtedness and penalize savings. We are taxed on interest earned, but interest paid on a home mortgage is a tax deduction. However, the Bible encourages savings and discourages debt. Our purpose is simply to challenge you to seek Christ with an open heart to learn what He wants you to do.

For Bev and me, this turned into an exciting time as we began to pay off our mortgage. The Lord provided additional funds for us in an unexpected way, and today we do not owe anyone anything. This allowed me to take time off from my job to study and develop the Crown materials. God may have something similar for you. Our living costs are more modest now than they were before, because we do not have debt or house payments.

The Bible encourages savings and discourages debt.

INVESTMENT DEBT

Should you borrow money to make an investment? In our opinion, it is permissible to borrow for an investment but only if you are not personally required to guarantee repayment of the debt. The investment for which you borrow (and any money invested as a down payment) should be the sole collateral for the debt. At first this may appear to contradict the biblical instruction for godly people to repay their debts. But let's explore this issue further.

For example, if we wanted to purchase a $70,000 rental house with $15,000 as the down payment, we would submit a loan application specifying the requirement of the house as sole security for the debt. We would explain to the lender that if, for any reason, we were unable to repay the loan, we would lose the $15,000 down payment, plus any other money we invested in the house, and the lender would own the house.

The lender must then make a business decision. Is a sufficient down payment invested? Is the house valuable enough? Is the housing market strong enough for the lender to feel secure about making the loan? In our opinion, the only circumstance under which we can be freed from the personal responsibility for a debt is when we have clearly communicated with the lender before obtaining the loan that we are not personally guaranteeing repayment of the loan.

Some have responded that it is impossible to locate a lender willing to loan without a personal guarantee. However, many later admitted they had not made a sincere effort to obtain such a loan. We repeatedly have seen the Lord allow His children to obtain this type of financing as they made this an object of prayer.

Be sure to limit your potential loss to the money you invested and the investment itself, because of the possibility of difficult financial events over which you have no control. It is painful to lose your investment, but it is much more serious to risk all your assets on investment debt. This position may appear too conservative. However, many people have become slaves of the lender and lost everything by guaranteeing debt on investments that went sour.

BUSINESS DEBT

We also want to encourage you to pray about becoming debt free in your business. Many are beginning to pay off all business-related debts, which helps establish a more financially stable enterprise.

CHURCH DEBT

Scripture does not specifically address whether a church may borrow money to build or expand its facility. In our opinion, such debt is permissible if the church leadership clearly senses the leading of the Lord to do so. If a church borrows, we recommend that it raise as much money as possible for the down payment and establish a plan to pay off the debt as rapidly as possible. A growing number of churches have chosen to build without the use of any debt. For many of these churches, the members have been encouraged and their faith increased as they have observed the Lord providing the necessary funds.

Godly people should pay their debts and bills as promptly as they can.

Prompt Payment

Many delay payments to creditors until payments are past due, even when they have the money. This, however, is not biblical. Proverbs 3:27-28 reads, *"Do not withhold good from those to whom it is due, when it is in your power to do it. Do not say to your neighbor, 'Go, and come back, and tomorrow I will give it,' when you have it with you."*

Godly people should pay their debts and bills as promptly as they can. Some have a policy of trying to pay each bill the same day they receive it to demonstrate to others that knowing Jesus Christ has made them financially responsible.

Using Your Savings

In our opinion, it is wise not to use all your savings to pay off debt. Maintain a reasonable level of savings to provide for the unexpected. If you apply all your savings against debt and the unexpected occurs, you will probably be forced back into debt to fund the emergency.

Bankruptcy

A court can declare a person bankrupt and unable to pay his or her debts. Depending on the type of bankruptcy, the court will either allow the debtor to develop a plan to repay his creditors or the court will distribute that person's property among the creditors as payment for the debts.

A wave of bankruptcy is sweeping our country. Should a godly person declare bankruptcy? The answer is generally no. Psalm 37:21 tells us, *"The wicked borrows and does not pay back."*

However, in our opinion, bankruptcy is permissible under two circumstances: a creditor forces a person into bankruptcy, or counselors believe the debtor's emotional health is at stake because of inability to cope with the pressure of creditors. For example, a husband may desert his wife and children, leaving her with business and family bills and debts for which she is responsible. She may not have the resources to meet those obligations. The emotional trauma of an unwanted divorce, coupled with harassment from unsympathetic creditors, may be too much to bear.

After a person goes through bankruptcy, he or she should seek counsel from an attorney to determine if it's legally permissible to attempt to repay the debt even though there is no obligation to do so. If it is allowable, every effort should be made to repay the debt. For a large debt, this may be a long-term goal that largely depends on the Lord's supernatural provision.

COSIGNING

Cosigning relates to debt. Anytime you cosign, you become legally responsible for the debt of another. It is just as if you went to the bank, borrowed the money and gave it to your friend or relative who is asking you to cosign.

A Federal Trade Commission study found that 50 percent of those who cosigned for bank loans ended up making the payment. Seventy-five percent of those who cosigned for finance company loans ended up making the payments! Unfortunately, few cosigners plan for this. The casualty rate is so high because the lender has already determined that the loan is a bad risk. That is why the lender won't make the loan without someone who is financially responsible to guarantee its repayment.

Fortunately, Scripture speaks clearly about cosigning. Proverbs 17:18 says, *"It is poor judgment to countersign another's note, to become responsible for his debts"* (TLB). The words "poor judgment" are better translated "destitute of mind"!

A parent often cosigns for his or her child's first automobile. The Watsons decided not to do this. They wanted to model for their children the importance of not cosigning and to discourage them from using debt. Instead, they trained them to plan ahead and save for the cash purchase of their first cars.

If you have already cosigned for a loan, the Scripture gives you counsel. Proverbs 6:1-5 says, *"Son, if you endorse a note for someone you hardly know, guaranteeing his debt, you are in serious trouble. You may have trapped yourself by your agreement. Quick! Get out of it if you possibly can! Swallow your pride; don't let embarrassment stand in the way. Go and beg to have your name erased. Don't put it off. . . . If you can get out of this trap you have saved yourself like a deer that escapes from a hunter, or a bird from the net"* (TLB).

Please use sound judgment and never cosign.

D E B T   N O T E S

COUNSEL

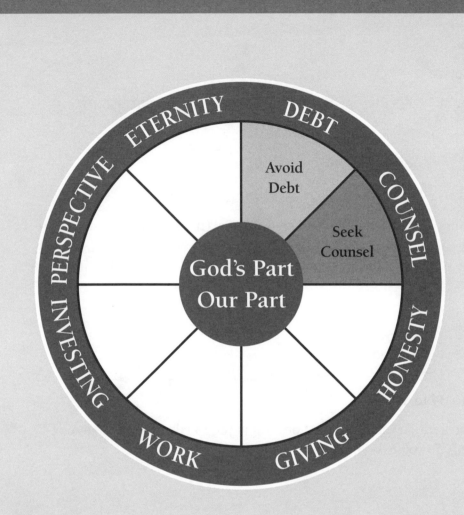

A Wise Person Seeks Advice

*"The way of a fool is right in his own eyes,
but a wise man is he who listens to counsel"*
(Proverbs 12:15).

Scripture to Memorize

"The way of a fool is right in his own eyes, but a wise man is he who listens to counsel" (Proverbs 12:15).

Practical Application: ☐ Complete the Estimated Budget. (If you prefer to use a computer budgeting program, we suggest installing the *Money Matters* software FREE 30-Day Trial located on the *Practical Application Workbook CD*. This is a special offer to Crown *Biblical Financial Study* attendees.)

DAY ONE

Read the Debt Notes on pages 34 to 45.

1. Are you in debt? If so, what steps do you sense the Lord wants you to take to become free of debt? If not, what safeguards do you have in place to help you remain debt free?

2. What did you learn about debt that proved to be especially helpful?

COUNSEL

Read *Proverbs 12:15; Proverbs 13:10; and Proverbs 15:22.*

1. What are some of the benefits of seeking counsel?

  Proverbs 12:15—

  Proverbs 13:10—

  Proverbs 15:22—

2. What are some of the benefits you have experienced from seeking counsel?

3. What hinders you from seeking counsel?

COUNSEL

Read *Psalm 16:7* **and** *Psalm 32:8*.

1. Does the Lord actively counsel His children? How?

Read *Psalm 106:13-15*.

2. What was the consequence of not seeking the Lord's counsel in this passage?

3. Have you ever suffered for not seeking the Lord's counsel? If so, describe what happened.

DAY FOUR

Read *Psalm 119:24; Psalm 119:105; 2 Timothy 3:16-17;* **and** *Hebrews 4:12*.

1. Should the Bible also serve as your counselor? Why?

COUNSEL

Read *Psalm 119:98-100*.

2. Living by the counsel of Scripture—

■ Makes us wiser than:

■ Gives us more insight than:

■ Gives us more understanding than:

3. Do you consistently read and study the Bible? If not, what prevents your consistency?

DAY FIVE

Read *Proverbs 1:8-9*.

1. Who should be among your counselors?

2. In your opinion, who should be the number-one human counselor of a husband? Of a wife? Why?

Read *Proverbs 11:14* **and** *Ecclesiastes 4:9-12.*

3. What do these verses communicate to you?

   Proverbs 11:14—

   Ecclesiastes 4:9-12—

4. How do you propose to apply this principle in your personal and/or business life?

DAY SIX

Read *Psalm 1:1-3.*

1. Whom should you avoid as a counselor?

2. What is your definition of a wicked person?

Read *Proverbs 12:5*.

3. Why should you avoid that counsel?

4. Is there ever a circumstance in which you should seek the input of a person who does not know Christ? If so, when?

 Please write your prayer requests in your Prayer Log before coming to class.

 I will take the following action as a result of this week's study.

C O U N S E L

COUNSEL NOTES 👑

Please do not read these notes until you have completed the Counsel Homework.

COUNSEL NOTES

I frequently counsel people who have financial problems. Often, they could have avoided their difficulties if they had sought counsel from someone with a solid understanding of God's perspective of money.

SEEKING COUNSEL

"Listen to advice and accept instruction, and in the end you will be wise"

PROVERBS 19:20 (NIV)

Two attitudes keep us from seeking counsel. The first one is pride. Our culture perceives seeking advice as a sign of weakness. We are told, "Stand on your own two feet. You don't need anyone to help make your decisions for you!" Advertisers subtly encourage this because they know that the impulse sale often will be lost if the purchaser takes time to seek counsel. Second, is the attitude of stubbornness. This attitude is characterized by the statement, "Don't confuse me with the facts. My mind is already made up!" We often resist seeking counsel because we do not want to learn the financial facts another person might discover. We don't want to be told we can't afford what we already have decided to buy.

God encourages us to use a great gift He has provided for our benefit—godly counselors. In Proverbs 19:20 we read, *"Listen to advice and accept instruction, and in the end you will be wise"* (NIV). Proverbs 12:15 says, *"The way of a fool is right in his own eyes, but a wise man is he who listens to counsel."* And Proverbs 10:8 says: *"The wise man is glad to be instructed, but a self-sufficient fool falls flat on his face"* (TLB).

One seeks counsel to secure insights, suggestions, and alternatives that will aid in making a proper decision. It is not the counselor's role to make the decision. You retain that responsibility.

Gather facts, but. . . .

We need to assemble the facts that will influence our decisions, but we also need to seek God's direction as well. We must determine specifically what the Lord wants us to do, and this may be contrary to what the facts alone would dictate.

This is illustrated in Numbers 13 and 14. Moses sent twelve spies into the Promised Land. All of the spies came back with an identical assessment of the facts: It was a prosperous land, but terrifying giants lived there. Only two of the twelve spies, Joshua and Caleb, believed what the Lord wanted them to do: go in and possess the Promised Land. Because the children of Israel relied only on the facts and did not act in faith on what the Lord wanted for them, they suffered 40 years of wandering in the wilderness until the entire generation had died.

SOURCES OF COUNSEL

What are the sources of counsel we need to seek? Before making a financial decision, particularly an important one, subject the decision to three sources of counsel.

THE COUNSEL OF SCRIPTURE

First, what does God's Word say about a particular issue? The Psalmist wrote, *"Your laws are both my light and my counselors"* (Psalm 119:24, TLB).

> *"Your commands make me wiser than my enemies. . . . I have more insight than all my teachers, for I meditate on your statutes"* (Psalm 119:98-99, NIV). *"I understand more than the aged, because I have observed Your precepts"* (Psalm 119:100, NASB).

When we think of people who are skilled in financial decision making, we often think of experts or those who are older and more experienced. Yet Scripture tells us we can have more insight and more wisdom than those who are educated and experienced in the ways of the world's economy by searching the Bible. I would rather obey the truth of Scripture than risk suffering the consequences of following my own inclinations or the opinions of people.

The Bible makes this remarkable claim about itself: *"For the word of God is living and active and sharper than any two-edged sword, and . . . able to judge the thoughts and intentions of the heart"* (Hebrews 4:12). The truths in the Bible are timeless. It is a living book that our Lord uses to communicate His direction to all generations.

It may have come as a surprise to you to learn that the Bible contains 2,350 verses dealing with how we should handle money. The very first filter we should put a financial decision through is Scripture. If the Scriptures answer a question, we do not have to go any further, because the Bible contains the Lord's written, revealed will.

Bob and Barbara were faced with a difficult decision. Barbara's brother and his wife had just moved to Florida from Chicago. Because they experienced financial difficulties in Chicago, the bank would not lend them the money to purchase a home unless they had someone cosign the debt. They asked Bob and Barbara to cosign. Barbara pleaded for Bob to do so; however, he was reluctant.

A friend referred them to the verses that warn against cosigning. When Barbara read the passages she responded, "Who am I to argue with God? We shouldn't cosign." Bob was tremendously relieved.

Two years later, Barbara's brother and his wife were divorced and he declared bankruptcy. Can you imagine the strain on their marriage if Bob had cosigned? He might have said, "Barbara, I can't believe your brother did this! You got me into this! I tried not to cosign but you forced me!" They probably would not have been able to survive financially.

The Bible makes a remarkable claim about itself: "For the word of God is living and active and sharper than any two-edged sword, and . . . able to judge the thoughts and intentions of the heart" (Hebrews 4:12).

COUNSEL NOTES

"Dear Lord, let me be the big cheese in the number-one job of the top outfit in the country, and let me come up with the right answers at the right times in the right places, but with it all, let me remain softspoken, country-shy, plain old Jeff Crotts from Spikard, Missouri."

If the Bible provides clear direction in a financial matter, we know what to do. If the Bible is not specific about an issue, we should subject our decision to the second source of counsel: godly people.

THE COUNSEL OF GODLY PEOPLE

"The godly man is a good counselor because he is just and fair and knows right from wrong" (Psalm 37:30-31, TLB). The Christian life is not one of independence from other Christians but of interdependence on one other. This is illustrated clearly in Paul's discussion concerning the body of Christ in 1 Corinthians 12. Each of us is pictured as a different member of this body. Our ability to function most effectively is dependent on the members working together. God has given each of us certain abilities and gifts, but God has not given any one person all the abilities that he or she needs to be most productive.

Spouse

If you are married, the first person you need to consult is your spouse. Frankly, it has been a humbling experience for me to seek the counsel of my wife Bev in financial matters, because she has no formal financial training. But she has saved us a great deal of money by her wise counsel.

Women tend to be gifted with a wonderfully sensitive and intuitive nature that is usually very accurate. Men tend to focus more objectively on the facts. The husband and wife need each other to achieve the proper balance for a correct decision. I believe that the Lord honors the wife's "office" or "position" as helpmate to her husband. Many times the Lord communicates most clearly to the husband through his wife.

If you are a husband, let me be blunt. Regardless of her business background or her financial aptitude, you must cultivate and seek your wife's counsel. I have committed never to proceed with a financial decision unless Bev agrees. There are additional benefits from seeking your spouse's counsel.

■ **It will preserve your relationship!**
The husband and wife should agree, because they both will experience the consequences of the decision. Even if their choice proves to be disastrous, their relationship remains intact. There are no grounds for an "I told you so" response.

■ **It will honor your spouse and prepare him or her for the future.**
Unfortunately, some in our culture suffer from a feeling of not being valuable. Seeking your spouse's counsel will help enormously in the development of a healthy and proper self-esteem. When a husband or wife seeks the other's advice, he or she actually is communicating, "I love you. I respect you. I value your insight." Consistently asking for advice also keeps your spouse informed of your

true financial condition. This is important in the event you predecease your spouse or are unable to work. My father suffered a massive heart attack that incapacitated him for two years. Because he kept my mother informed about his business, she was able to step in and operate it successfully until he recovered.

Parents

The second source of counsel is our parents.

> *"My son, observe the commandment of your father and do not forsake the teaching of your mother; bind them continually on your heart; tie them around your neck. When you walk about, they will guide you; when you sleep, they will watch over you; and when you awake, they will talk to you"* (Proverbs 6:20-22).

Our parents have the benefit of years of experience, and they know us so well. In our opinion, we should seek their counsel even if they do not yet know Christ or have not been wise money managers themselves. Over the years, it's not uncommon for a barrier to be erected between a child and parents. Asking their advice is a way to honor our parents and to build a bridge across any wall. It is a compliment for anyone to ask your advice—an expression of admiration. A word of caution: Although the husband and wife should seek the counsel of their parents, the advice of the parents should be subordinate to the advice of the spouse, especially if a family conflict materializes.

"Now remember, John, no honey until you've finished all your locusts."

> *"A man shall leave his father and his mother, and shall be joined to his wife; and they shall become one flesh"* (Genesis 2:24, NIV).

Experienced People

We should also consult people experienced in the area in which we are attempting to make a decision. If you are considering a real estate investment, attempt to locate the most qualified real estate investor to counsel you. If you are going to purchase a car, ask a trustworthy automobile mechanic to examine the car and give you an opinion before purchasing it.

A Multitude of Counselors

We read in Proverbs 15:22, *"Without consultation, plans are frustrated, but with many counselors they succeed."* And Proverbs 11:14 says, *"Where there is no guidance the people fall, but in abundance of counselors there is victory."* Each of us has limited knowledge and experience; we need the input of others who bring their own unique backgrounds to broaden our thinking with alternatives we would never have considered without their advice.

I meet regularly with a small group who share their lives with one another and pray for each other. The members of this group know each other well. Over the years, each person has experienced a difficult circumstance or had to make a major decision. We have learned that when someone is subjected to a painful circumstance, it is difficult to make wise, dispassionate decisions. We have experienced the benefits and safety of having a group of people who love one another, who know one another, and who can give objective counsel even when

Each of us has limited knowledge and experience; we need the imput of others, who bring their own unique backgrounds to broaden our thinking with alternatives.

it hurts. We are more receptive to constructive criticism when it comes from someone who cares for us.

We also have learned that a major advantage of this close relationship is
that we know each other's weaknesses and strengths. Because of this, it is easier to discern what direction the one seeking counsel should pursue. Solomon
describes the benefits of interdependence upon one another:

> *"Two are better than one because they have a good return for their
> labor. For if either of them falls, the one will lift up his compan-
> ion. But woe to the one who falls when there is not another to lift
> him up. Furthermore, if two lie down together they keep warm,
> but how can one be warm alone? And if one can overpower him
> who is alone, two can resist him. A cord of three strands is not
> quickly torn apart"* (Ecclesiastes 4:9-12).

It can be very productive to gather your counselors together. Frequently
the suggestions of one will trigger insights from another. What one says can
be confirmed or discussed by the others. It is not uncommon for a clear direction to be established when all of your counselors gather together.

When seeking a multitude of counselors, they often will not offer the
same recommendations; in fact, there can be sharp disagreement. But usually a common thread will begin to develop, or sometimes each counselor
will supply you with a different insight you need to help you make the decision.

We encourage you to include your pastor among your counselors, particularly when you are faced with a major decision.

THE COUNSEL OF THE LORD

During the process of analyzing the facts, searching the Bible, and obtaining
the counsel of godly people, we need to be seeking direction from the Lord.
This is the most important thing we can do. In Isaiah 9:6 we are told that one
of the Lord's names is *"Wonderful Counselor."*

The Psalms also identify the Lord as our counselor. *"I [the Lord] will instruct
you and teach you in the way which you should go; I will counsel you with My
eye upon you"* (Psalm 32:8). *"You [the Lord] guide me with your counsel"* (Psalm
73:24, NIV). *"I will bless the Lord who has counseled me"* (Psalm 16:7).

In Scripture there are numerous examples of the unfortunate consequences of not seeking God's counsel and the blessings of heeding His
counsel. After the children of Israel began their campaign to capture the
Promised Land, some of the natives (Gibeonites) attempted to enter into a
peace treaty with Israel. The Gibeonites deceived the leaders of Israel into
believing they were from a distant land. Joshua 9:14-15 reads, *"The men of
Israel took some of their [Gibeonites'] provisions, and **did not ask for the counsel of the Lord**. Joshua made peace with them and made a covenant with them,
to let them live"* [emphasis mine].

The consequence of not seeking the Lord's counsel was that the Promised
Land remained populated with ungodly people and Israel became ensnared
by their false gods. The leaders were influenced by the "facts" they could see—

facts that were designed to deceive them into thinking that the Gibeonites lived far away. In many situations only the Lord can reveal to us real truth and proper direction. Only the Lord knows the future and the ultimate outcome of a decision.

A wonderful contrast is found in John 21:3-11. Peter and six of the other disciples fished all night long but caught nothing. Jesus then came to the seashore and instructed them to cast their net once again. They obeyed and caught 153 large fish. When we know what Christ wants us to do and we obey, it is much more productive than our efforts apart from His direction.

Throughout Scripture we are encouraged to wait on the Lord. Whenever you feel hurried or pressured or you are confused concerning a decision, go to a quiet place that will allow you to listen quietly for His still, small voice. The world around you screams "Hurry!" but our loving heavenly Father's advice is worth waiting for.

COUNSEL TO AVOID

AVOIDING THE COUNSEL OF THE WICKED

We need to avoid one particular source of counsel. *"How blessed is the man who does not walk in the counsel of the wicked"* (Psalm 1:1). The word "blessed" literally means to be "happy many times over." The definition of a "wicked" person is one who lives his or her life without regard to God. A wicked person can be a person who does not yet personally know the Lord or one who knows Jesus Christ as Savior but is not following Him in obedience. Avoid the counsel of the wicked.

In our opinion, when you are searching for facts or technical expertise, you may seek input from those who may not know Christ. Then after considering their input, you are responsible to make the final decision.

Fortune Tellers, Mediums, and Spiritualists

The Bible bluntly tells us never to seek the advice of fortune tellers, mediums, or spiritualists: *"Do not turn to mediums or seek out spiritists, for you will be defiled by them. I am the Lord your God"* (Leviticus 19:31, NIV). Study this next passage carefully: *"Saul died because he was unfaithful to the Lord . . . and even consulted a medium for guidance and did not inquire of the Lord. So the Lord put him to death"* (1 Chronicles 10:13-14, NIV). Saul died, in part, because he went to a medium. We should also avoid anything they use in forecasting the future, such as horoscopes and all other practices of the occult.

Biased Counsel

We need to be cautious of the counsel of the biased. When receiving financial advice, ask yourself this question: "What stake does this person have in the outcome of my decision? Does he or she stand to gain or lose from this decision?" If the advisor will profit, be cautious when evaluating this counsel and always seek a second unbiased opinion.

Throughout Scripture we are encouraged to wait upon the Lord. Whenever you feel hurried or pressured or you are confused concerning a decision, go to a quiet place that will allow you to listen quietly for His still, small voice.

GROW UP...QUIT WHINING...GET OUTTA HERE.

When you are seeking advice, supply your counselor with all the important facts. Do not attempt to manipulate your advisor to give the answer you want by concealing information.

Major Decisions

Whenever you are faced with a major decision, such as a job change or home purchase, it is very helpful to go to a quiet place where you can spend uninterrupted time praying, reading Scripture, and seeking the Lord's direction. We encourage you to consider fasting during this time.

Know Your Counselors

Be selective in choosing your counselors. Make sure they have the courage to give you advice that may be contrary to your wishes, and attempt to include those who are gifted with wisdom. *"He who walks with the wise grows wise"* (Proverbs 13:20, NIV).

Continually ask the Lord for wisdom. *"If any of you lacks wisdom, let him ask of God, who gives to all . . . and it will be given to him. But let him ask in faith without any doubting"* (James 1:5-6).

As you seek counsel, do not be surprised if the answer comes out of your own mouth. Interacting with others allows you to verbalize thoughts and feelings that you may never have expressed clearly.

Counseling others can be a frustrating experience, unless you understand the proper role of the counselor. Simply stated, the counselor should lovingly communicate the truth to the person seeking counsel, to the best of his or her ability, and leave the results to God. In the past I often became involved emotionally in whether people would act on my recommendations. However, I discovered that some people are not yet prepared to follow advice. At other times I would discover later that my counsel was inaccurate or incomplete. The counselor needs to be content, knowing that the Lord is in control of every counseling experience.

Observe Strict Confidentiality

The person seeking advice needs to know that nothing he or she says will be communicated to another person without permission. Only in an environment of trust will there be the candid dialogue that produces successful results.

When You Do Not Know

When you are asked a question you do not know, you must be careful not to fabricate an answer. Simply respond: "I do not know." Often people come with

Simply stated, the counselor should lovingly communicate the truth to the person seeking counsel, to the best of his or her ability, and leave the results to God.

COUNSEL NOTES

problems or circumstances that are outside of our experience. The best way to serve is to refer them to someone who has expertise in his or her area of need.

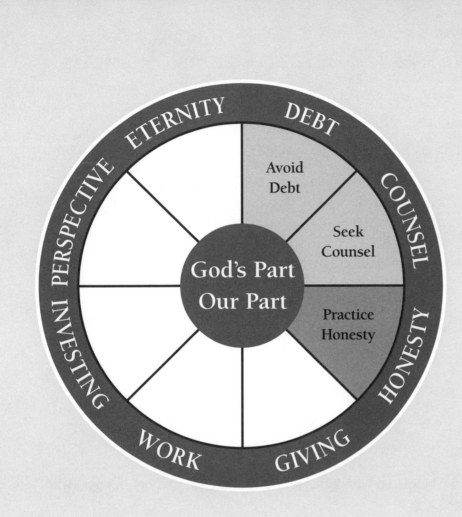

God's Standard Is Absolute

*"You shall not steal, nor deal falsely,
nor lie to one another"*
(Leviticus 19:11).

HONESTY HOMEWORK ♛

Scripture to Memorize

"You shall not steal, nor deal falsely, nor lie to one another" (Leviticus 19:11).

Practical Application: □ Complete the Adjusting Your Budget practical application.

DAY ONE

Read the Counsel Notes on pages 54 to 61.

1. What elements of God's perspective of counsel especially interested you?

2. Do you actively seek counsel when faced with a major financial decision? If not, how do you propose to do so in the future?

Read *Leviticus 19:11-13; Deuteronomy 25:13-16; Ephesians 4:25;* **and** *1 Peter 1:15-16.*

1. What do these verses communicate to you about God's demand for honesty?

    Leviticus 19:11-13 —

    Deuteronomy 25:13-16 —

    Ephesians 4:25 —

    1 Peter 1:15-16 —

2. Are you consistently honest in even the smallest details? If not, what will you do to change?

3. What are two factors that motivate or influence us to act dishonestly?

    ■

    ■

4. How does this apply to you?

HONESTY

Read *Exodus 18:21-22*.

1. Does the Lord require honesty for leaders? Why?

Then read *Proverbs 28:16* **and** *Proverbs 29:12*.

2. What are the consequences of dishonesty for people in leadership?

    Proverbs 28:16 —

    Proverbs 29:12 —

3. How does this apply to you?

DAY FOUR

Read *Proverbs 14:2*.

1. Can you practice dishonesty and still love God? Why?

Read *Proverbs 26:28* **and** *Romans 13:9-10*.

2. According to these passages, can you practice dishonesty and still love your neighbor? Why?

Read *Psalm 15:1-5; Proverbs 12:22; Proverbs 20:7;* **and** *Isaiah 33:15-16.*

1. What are some of the benefits of honesty?

    Psalm 15:1-5 —

    Proverbs 12:22 —

    Proverbs 20:7 —

    Isaiah 33:15-16 —

Read *Proverbs 3:32; Proverbs 13:11;* **and** *Proverbs 21:6.*

2. What are some of the curses of dishonesty?

    Proverbs 3:32 —

    Proverbs 13:11 —

    Proverbs 21:6 —

HONESTY

Read *Exodus 22:1-4; Numbers 5:5-8; and Luke 19:8.*

1. What does the Bible say about restitution?

2. If you have acquired anything dishonestly, how will you make restitution?

Read *Exodus 23:8; Proverbs 15:27; and Proverbs 29:4.*

3. What does Scripture say about bribes?

4. Have you ever been asked to give or take a bribe? If so, describe what happened.

 Please write your prayer requests in your Prayer Log before coming to class.

 I will take the following action as a result of this week's study.

HONESTY NOTES 👑

Please do not read these notes until you have completed the Honesty Homework.

All of us have to make daily decisions about whether or not to handle money honestly. Do we tell the cashier at the store when we receive too much change? Have you ever tried to sell something and been tempted not to tell the whole truth because you might have lost the sale?

HONESTY IN SOCIETY

People today formulate their own standards of honesty, which change, depending on their circumstances.

These decisions are made more difficult because everyone around us seems to be acting dishonestly. After pumping five dollars' worth of gas in my truck, I asked for a receipt, and the attendant made the receipt for ten dollars. When I pointed out the mistake, he replied, "Oh, just turn in the receipt to your company and you'll make a fast five bucks. After all, that's what many of the mail deliverers do in this area."

When I heard that, my heart sank. The verse that came immediately to mind was Judges 17:6, *"Every man did what was right in his own eyes."* People today formulate their own standards of honesty, which change, depending on their circumstances.

HONESTY IN SCRIPTURE

There are hundreds of verses in the Bible that communicate the Lord's desire for us to be completely honest. For instance, Proverbs 20:23 reads, *"The Lord loathes all cheating and dishonesty"* (TLB). And Proverbs 12:22 states, *"Lying lips are an abomination to the Lord."* And in Proverbs 6:16-17 we read, *"The Lord hates . . . a lying tongue."*

Study the following comparison between what the Scriptures teach and what our society practices concerning honesty.

Issue	Scripture	Society
Standard of honesty	Absolute	Relative
God's concern about honesty	He demands honesty	There is no God
The decision to be honest or dishonest is based on	Faith in the invisible, living God	Only the facts that can be seen
Question usually asked when deciding whether to be honest	Will it please God?	Will I get away with it?

The God of Truth

Truthfulness is one of God's characteristics. He is repeatedly identified as the God of truth. *"I am . . . the truth"* (John 14:6). And the Lord commands us to reflect His honest and holy character: *"Be holy yourselves also in all your behavior; because it is written, 'You shall be holy, for I am holy'"* (1 Peter 1:15-16).

In contrast to God's nature, John 8:44 describes the devil's character:

> *"He* [the devil] *was a murderer from the beginning, and does not stand in the truth because there is no truth in him. When-ever he speaks a lie, he speaks from his own nature, for he is a liar and the father of lies."*

The Lord wants us to become conformed to His honest character rather than to the dishonest nature of the devil.

ABSOLUTE HONESTY

God wants us to be totally honest for the following reasons.

We Cannot Practice Dishonesty and Love God

Two of the Ten Commandments address honesty. *"You shall not steal. You shall not bear false witness against your neighbor"* (Exodus 20:15-16). And Jesus told us, *"If you love Me, you will keep My commandments"* (John 14:15).

We cannot disobey by practicing dishonesty and still love God. When being dishonest, we are acting as if the living God doesn't even exist! We believe that God is not able to provide exactly what we need, even though He has promised to do so (Matthew 6:33). We decide to take things into our own hands and do it our own dishonest way. We are also acting as if God is incapable of discovering our dishonesty and is powerless to discipline us. If we really believe God will discipline us, then we will not consider acting dishonestly.

When being dishonest, we are acting as if the living God doesn't even exist! We believe that God is not able to provide exactly what we need, even though He has promised to do so.

Honest behavior is an issue of faith. An honest decision may look foolish in light of what we can see, but the godly person knows Jesus Christ is alive, even though invisible. Every honest decision strengthens our faith in God and helps us grow into a closer relationship with Christ. However, if we choose to be dishonest, we are really denying our Lord. It is impossible to love God with all our hearts, souls, and minds if, at the same time, we are dishonest and act as if He does not exist. Scripture declares that the dishonest hate God.

> *He who walks in his uprightness fears the Lord, but he who is devious [crooked] in his ways despises Him"* (Proverbs 14:2).

This is a big issue to me because of my own experience. Before learning God's view of honesty, I was often dishonest in my financial dealings. However, once I began breaking my dishonest habits, I realized that the Lord wants us to be honest primarily so that we can experience a closer relationship with Him.

We Cannot Practice Dishonesty and Love Our Neighbor
The Lord requires honesty because dishonest behavior also violates the second commandment, *"You shall love your neighbor as yourself"* (Mark 12:31). Romans 13:9-10 reads, *"If you love your neighbor as much as you love yourself you will not want to harm or cheat him, or kill him or steal from him. . . . Love does no wrong to anyone"* (TLB).

When we act dishonestly, we are stealing from another person. We may deceive ourselves into thinking it is a business, the government, or an insurance company that is suffering loss, but really it is the business owners, fellow taxpayers, or policy holders from whom we are stealing. It is just as if we had taken the money from their wallets. Dishonesty always injures people. The victim is always a person.

Credibility for Evangelism
Our Lord requires honesty to enable us to demonstrate the reality of Jesus Christ to those who do not yet know Him.

I will never forget the first time I told a neighbor how he could come to know Christ as his personal Savior. He angrily responded, "Well, I know a man who always goes to church and talks a lot about Jesus, but watch out if you ever get in a business deal with him! He'd cheat his own grandmother! If that's what it means to be a Christian, I don't want any part of it!"

Our actions speak louder than our words.

> *"Prove yourselves to be blameless and innocent, children of God above reproach in the midst of a crooked and perverse generation, among whom you appear as lights in the world"* (Philippians 2:15).

We can influence people **for** Jesus Christ by handling our money honestly. Robert Newsom had been trying to sell a car for months. Finally, an interested buyer decided to purchase the car. However, at the last moment he said, "I'll buy this car, but only on one condition—you don't report this sale so I won't have to pay state sales tax."

"If you love your neighbor as much as you love yourself you will not want to harm or cheat him, or kill him or steal from him . . . love does no wrong to anyone" (Romans 13:9-10).

Although he was tempted, Robert responded, "I'm sorry, I can't do that because Jesus Christ is my Lord." Robert later said, "You should have seen the buyer's reaction. He almost went into shock! Then an interesting thing happened. His attitude completely changed. Not only did he purchase the car, but he eagerly joined my wife and me at our dinner table. Rarely have I seen anyone as open to the truth about knowing Jesus Christ in a personal way."

Because Robert had acted honestly, even though it was going to cost him money (*"Prove yourselves to be blameless and innocent, children of God above reproach"*), he had demonstrated to this person (*"a crooked and perverse generation"*) the reality of a personal faith in Jesus Christ (*"appear as lights in the world"*).

Confirms God's Direction

Proverbs 4:24-26 reads, *"Put away from you a deceitful mouth and put devious speech far from you. Let your eyes look directly ahead and let your gaze be fixed straight in front of you. Watch the path of your feet and all your ways will be established."* What a tremendous principle. As you are completely honest, *"all your ways will be established."* Choosing to walk the narrow path of honesty eliminates the many possible avenues of dishonesty. Decision making becomes simpler because the honest path is a clear path.

"If only I had understood that truth," Raymond wept. "But Donna and I wanted that house so much. However, our debts were so large that we couldn't qualify for the mortgage. The only way for us to buy the house was to hide some of our debts from the bank.

"It was the worst decision of my life. We were unable to meet the mortgage payment and pay our other debts too. The pressure built and was almost more than Donna could stand. Our dream house ended up causing a family nightmare. I not only lost the home but nearly lost my wife."

Had Raymond and Donna been honest, the bank would not have approved the loan. They would not have been able to purchase that particular home. Had they prayed and waited, perhaps the Lord would have brought something more affordable, thus avoiding the pressure that almost ended their marriage. Honesty helps confirm God's direction.

Even Small Acts of Dishonesty Are Harmful

God requires us to be **completely honest**, because even the smallest act of dishonesty is sin. And even the smallest sin interrupts our fellowship with the Lord and retards our maturity in Christ. The smallest "white lie" will harden our hearts, make our consciences increasingly insensitive to sin, and deafen our ears to the still small voice of the Lord. This single cancer cell of small dishonesty multiplies and spreads to greater dishonesty. *"Whoever is dishonest with very little will also be dishonest with much"* (Luke 16:10, NIV).

An event in Abraham's life challenges us to be honest in small matters. In Genesis 14 the king of Sodom offered Abraham all the goods Abraham recovered when he successfully rescued the people of Sodom. But Abraham responded to the king, *"I have sworn to the Lord God Most High, possessor of*

Choosing to walk the narrow path of honesty eliminates the many possible avenues of dishonesty. Decision making becomes simpler because the honest path is a clear path.

heaven and earth, that I will not take a thread or a sandal thong or anything that is yours" (Genesis 14:22-23).

Just as Abraham was unwilling to take so much as a thread, we challenge you to make a similar commitment in this area of honesty. Covenant not to steal a stamp or a photocopy or a paper clip or a long distance telephone call or a penny from your employer, the government, or anyone else. The people of God must be honest in even the smallest matters.

To love God and our neighbors, to evangelize effectively, to confirm God's direction and to develop a heart sensitive to God—is there any wonder that our Lord knows it is best for us to be completely honest?

ESCAPING THE TEMPTATION OF DISHONESTY

A friend was teaching these principles in a secular school when one young man raised his hand and said, "I think we all would like to be the person you're talking about, but I know in my heart that if the right opportunity comes along, I'm going to be dishonest." I think he is correct. Apart from living our lives yielded to the Holy Spirit, all of us will be dishonest.

> *"Live by the Spirit, and you will not gratify the desires of the sinful nature. For the sinful nature desires what is contrary to the Spirit, and the Spirit what is contrary to the sinful nature"* (Galatians 5:16-17, NIV).

The character of our human nature is to act dishonestly. *"Out of men's hearts, come evil thoughts . . . theft . . . deceit"* (Mark 7:21-22, NIV). The desire of the Spirit is for us to be totally honest. The absolutely honest life is supernatural. We need to submit ourselves entirely to Jesus Christ as Lord and allow Him to live His life through us. There is no other way.

We heartily recommend you read a short book by Andrew Murray titled *Humility*. It is an excellent study for living your life yielded to Christ as Lord.

The following principles will help you to develop the habit of honesty.

1. By Practicing the Golden Rule

"Do not merely look out for your own personal interests, but also for the interests of others" (Philippians 2:4). This verse is better translated, "look intently" after the interests of others. The Lord used this passage to point out Warren's lack of concern for others just when he was about to purchase some land. The seller knew nothing of its value. Warren had been secretly congratulating himself because he knew the purchase price he was offering was very low. Not once had he even considered what would be fair to the seller. He had concentrated solely on acquiring the property at the lowest possible price.

Warren reexamined the transaction in the light of "looking intently" after the seller's interests as well as his own. After an intense inner struggle, he concluded that he should pay more for the property to reflect its true value. Practicing the Golden Rule is sometimes costly, but its reward is a clear conscience before God and other people.

Covenant not to steal a stamp or a photocopy or a paper clip or a long distance telephone call or a penny from your employer, the government, or anyone else. The people of God must be honest in even the smallest matters.

2. By a Healthy Fear of the Lord

When we talk of a "healthy fear" of the Lord, we do not mean that God is a big bully just waiting for the opportunity to punish us. Rather, He is a loving Father who, out of infinite love, disciplines His children for their benefit. *"He disciplines us for our good, so that we may share His holiness"* (Hebrews 12:10).

One of the methods God uses to motivate us to honest living is this "healthy fear." Proverbs 16:6 says, *"By the fear of the Lord one keeps away from evil."* John once shared a motel room with a friend. As they were leaving, his friend slipped one of the motel's towels into his suitcase and walked to the car. Suddenly, John felt the fear of the Lord. What came to mind was Hebrews 12:11, *"All discipline for the moment seems not to be joyful, but sorrowful."* Discipline hurts! John was afraid for his friend and for himself as an accomplice. Given the choice, we should obey His Word rather than to make a deliberate decision that will prompt our loving Father to discipline us. You can imagine how relieved John was when his friend returned the motel's towel!

Moreover, we believe our heavenly Father will not allow us to keep anything we have acquired dishonestly. Proverbs 13:11 reads, *"Wealth obtained by fraud dwindles."*

A friend purchased four azalea plants, but the check-out clerk had only charged her for one. She knew it, but she left the store anyway without paying for the other three. She told me it was miraculous how quickly three of those plants died! Think about this for a moment: If you are a parent and one of your children steals something, do you allow the child to keep it? Of course not, because the child's character would be destroyed if he or she kept stolen property. Not only do you insist on its return, but you usually want the child to experience enough discomfort to produce a lasting impression. For instance, you might have the child confess the theft to the store manager. When our heavenly Father lovingly disciplines us, it is usually done in such a way that we will not forget.

3. By Staying Away from Dishonest People

Scripture teaches that we are deeply influenced by those around us, either for good or for evil. David recognized this and said, *"My eyes shall be upon the faithful of the land, that they may dwell with me; he who walks in a blameless way is the one who will minister to me. He who practices deceit shall not dwell within my house; he who speaks falsehood shall not maintain his position before me"* (Psalm 101:6-7). Paul wrote, *"Do not be deceived: 'Bad company corrupts good morals'"* (1 Corinthians 15:33). Solomon was even stronger: *"He who is a partner with a thief hates his own life"* (Proverbs 29:24).

Obviously, we cannot isolate ourselves from every dishonest person. In fact, we are to be salt and light in the world. We should, however, be very cautious when choosing our close friends or considering a business relationship with another.

If I observe a person who is dishonest in dealing with the government or in a small matter, I know this person will be dishonest in greater matters and probably in dealing with me. In our opinion, it is impossible for a person to be selectively honest. Either the person has made the commitment to be

> Choosing to walk the narrow path of honesty eliminates the many possible avenues of dishonesty. Decision making becomes simpler because the honest path is a clear path.

absolutely honest or that person's dishonesty will become more prevalent. It is much easier to remain absolutely honest if you are surrounded by others who are of a like mind and conviction.

4. By Giving

We can escape the temptation of acting dishonestly by giving generously to those in need. *"He who steals must steal no longer; but rather he must labor, performing with his own hands what is good, so that he will have something to share with one who has need"* (Ephesians 4:28).

As we give, it draws us closer to Christ and reduces our incentive to steal. After all, if we are going to give something away, there's no reason to steal it!

WHAT TO DO WHEN WE HAVE BEEN DISHONEST

Unfortunately, from time to time, we will act dishonestly, but once we recognize that we have we need to do the following.

1. Restore Our Fellowship with God

Anytime we sin, we break our fellowship with our Lord, and this needs to be restored. First John 1:9 tells us how: *"If we confess our sins, He is faithful and righteous to forgive us our sins and to cleanse us from all unrighteousness."* We must agree with God that our dishonesty was sin and then thankfully accept God's gracious forgiveness so we can again enjoy His fellowship. Remember, God loves us. He is kind and merciful. God is ready to forgive our dishonesty when we turn from it.

2. Restore Our Fellowship with the Harmed Person

After our fellowship with Christ has been restored, we need to confess our dishonesty to the person we offended. *"Confess your sins to one another"* (James 5:16).

Ouch! This hurts. Only a handful of people have confessed that they have wronged me. Interestingly, these people have become some of my closest friends—in part because of my respect for them. They so desired an honest relationship that they were willing to expose their sins.

This has been very hard for me. For the first time, several years ago I went to someone I had wronged and confessed my sin—not that I hadn't had plenty of opportunities before! In the past, however, my pride stood in the way. Afterward I sensed a great freedom in our relationship. I also discovered that, because it is a painfully humbling experience, confession helps break the habit of dishonesty.

A person's lack of financial prosperity may be a consequence of violating this principle. *"He who conceals his transgressions will not prosper, but he who confesses and forsakes them will find compassion"* (Proverbs 28:13).

If I observe a person who is dishonest in dealing with the government or in a small matter, I know this person will be dishonest in greater matters and probably in dealing with me.

3. Restore Dishonestly Acquired Property

If we have acquired anything dishonestly, we must return it to its rightful owner. *"Then it shall be, when he sins and becomes guilty, that he shall restore what he took by robbery . . . or anything about which he swore falsely; he shall make restitution for it in full and add to it one-fifth more. He shall give it to the one to whom it belongs"* (Leviticus 6:4-5).

Restitution is a tangible expression of repentance and an effort to correct a wrong.

Restitution is a tangible expression of repentance and an effort to correct a wrong. Zaccheus is a good example. He promised Jesus, *"If I have defrauded anyone of anything, I will give back four times as much"* (Luke 19:8).

If it's not possible for restitution to be made, then the property should be given to the Lord. Numbers 5:8 teaches, *"If the man has no relative to whom restitution may be made for the wrong, the restitution which is made for the wrong must go to the Lord for the priest."*

HONESTY REQUIRED FOR LEADERS

The Lord is especially concerned with the honesty of leaders.

Influence of Leaders

Leaders influence those who follow them. The owner of a trucking business began wearing cowboy boots to work. Within six months, all the men in his office were in boots. He suddenly changed to traditional business shoes, and six months later all the men were wearing business shoes.

In a similar way, a dishonest leader produces dishonest followers. *"If a ruler pays attention to falsehood, all his ministers become wicked"* (Proverbs 29:12). The leader of a business, church, or home must set the example of honesty in his or her personal life before those under his or her authority can be expected to do the same.

The president of a large international construction company was asked why her company did not work in countries where bribes were a way of life. She responded, "We never build in those countries because we can't afford to. If my employees know we are acting dishonestly, they will eventually become thieves. Their dishonesty will ultimately cost us more than we could ever earn on a project."

During an effort to reduce expenses, a company discovered the employees were making frequent, personal, long-distance telephone calls at the office and charging them to the company. The company president had unwittingly fueled this problem. He had reasoned that because he placed approximately the same number of company long-distance calls on his home phone as personal long-distance calls on the company phone, a detailed accounting was unnecessary. His employees, however, knew only of his calls at work. They concluded that if this practice was acceptable for the boss it was acceptable for all. A leader should *"abstain from all appearance of evil"* (1 Thessalonians 5:22, KJV), because his or her actions influence others.

Selection of Leaders

Dishonesty should disqualify a person from leadership. Listen to the counsel of Jethro, Moses' father-in-law.

> *"You shall select out of all the people able men who fear God, men of truth, those who hate dishonest gain; and you shall place these . . . as leaders of thousands, of hundreds, of fifties and of tens"* (Exodus 18:21).

Two of the four criteria for leadership selection dealt with honesty: *"men of truth, those who hate dishonest gain."* We believe the Lord wants us to continue to select leaders on the basis of these same character qualities.

Preservation of Leaders

Not only are leaders selected in part by honest behavior, but a leader retains this position by honest behavior. *"A leader . . . who hates unjust gain will prolong his days"* (Proverbs 28:16). We have all witnessed the leaders of business or government who have been demoted because of a root problem of personal corruption.

How can a leader maintain the standard of absolute honesty? By becoming accountable. It is necessary to establish a system of checks and balances that do not usurp the leader's authority but which provide a structure to ensure that the leader is accountable.

BRIBES

A bribe is defined as anything given to influence a person to do something illegal or wrong. The taking of bribes is clearly prohibited in Scripture: *"You shall not take a bribe, for a bribe blinds the clear-sighted and subverts the cause of the just"* (Exodus 23:8). Bribes are often disguised as a "gift" or "referral fee." Evaluate any such offer to confirm that it is not in reality a bribe.

BLESSINGS AND CURSES

Listed on the next page are some of the blessings the Lord has promised for the honest and some of the curses reserved for the dishonest. Read these slowly and prayerfully, asking God to use His Word to motivate you to a life of honesty.

A leader should "abstain from all appearance of evil" (1 Thessalonians 5:22, KJV), because his or her actions influence others.

BLESSINGS FOR THE HONEST

- Blessing of a more intimate relationship with the Lord. *"The* [crooked] *are an abomination to the Lord; but He is intimate with the upright"* (Proverbs 3:32).

- Blessings on the family. *"A righteous man who walks in his integrity— how blessed are his sons after him"* (Proverbs 20:7).

- Blessings of life. *"Truthful lips will be established forever; but a lying tongue is only for a moment"* (Proverbs 12:19).

- Blessings of prosperity. *"Great wealth is in the house of the righteous, but trouble is in the income of the wicked"* (Proverbs 15:6).

CURSES RESERVED FOR THE DISHONEST

- Curse of alienation from God. *"The* [crooked] *are an abomination to the Lord"* (Proverbs 3:32).

- Curse on the family. *"He who profits illicitly troubles his own house, but he who hates bribes will live"* (Proverbs 15:27).

- Curse of death. *"The* [getting] *of treasures by a lying tongue is a fleeting vapor, the pursuit of death"* (Proverbs 21:6).

- Curse of poverty. *"Wealth obtained by fraud dwindles"* (Proverbs 13:11).

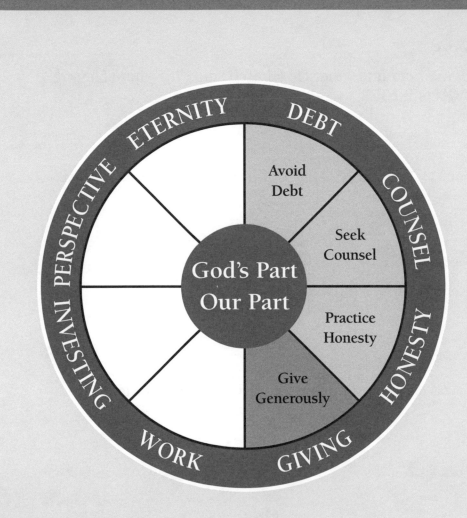

Giving Is Blessed

"Remember the words of the Lord Jesus, that He Himself said, 'It is more blessed to give than to receive'"
(Acts 20:35).

GIVING HOMEWORK

Homework To Be Completed for Week 6

Scripture to Memorize

"Remember the words of the Lord Jesus, that He Himself said, 'It is more blessed to give than to receive'" (Acts 20:35).

Practical Application: ☐ Complete the *Beginning Your Budget* practical application.

DAY ONE

Read the *Honesty Notes* on pages 69 to 78.

1. How does the example of Abraham in *Genesis 14:21-23* challenge you to be honest?

2. Ask the Lord to reveal any areas of dishonesty in your life. How do you propose to deal with these areas?

DAY TWO

Read *Matthew 23:23; 1 Corinthians 13:3;* and *2 Corinthians 9:7*.

1. What do these passages communicate about the importance of the proper attitude in giving?

   Matthew 23:23—

   1 Corinthians 13:3—

   2 Corinthians 9:7—

2. How do you think a person can develop the proper attitude in giving?

3. How would you describe your attitude in giving?

DAY THREE

Read *Acts 20:35.*

1. How does this principle from God's economy differ from the way most people view giving?

2. List the benefits for the giver that are found in each of the following passages.

Proverbs 11:24-25—

Matthew 6:20—

Luke 12:34—

1 Timothy 6:18-19—

Read *Malachi 3:8-10.*

1. Was the tithe (giving 10 percent) required under Old Testament Law?

Read *2 Corinthians 8:1-5.*

2. Identify three principles from this passage that should influence how much you give.

■

■

■

Prayerfully (with your spouse if you are married) seek the Lord's guidance to determine how much you should give. You will not be asked to disclose the amount.

Read *Numbers 18:8-10,24; Galatians 6:6; and 1 Timothy 5:17-18.*

1. What do these verses tell you about financially supporting your church and those who teach the Scriptures?

Numbers 18:8-10,24—

Galatians 6:6—

1 Timothy 5:17-18—

Read *Isaiah 58:6-11* **and** *Ezekiel 16:49*.

1. What do these verses say about giving to the poor?

    Isaiah 58:6-11—

    Ezekiel 16:49—

Read *Matthew 25:35-45*.

2. How does Jesus Christ identify with the needy?

Read *Galatians 2:9-10*.

3. What does this verse communicate to you about giving to the poor?

4. Are you currently giving to the needy? If not, what is hindering you?

 Please write your prayer requests in your Prayer Log before coming to class.

 I will take the following action as a result of this week's study.

GIVING NOTES 👑

Please do not read these notes until you have completed the Giving Homework.

Because God loved He gave. Because God is love, He is also a giver.

Few areas of the Christian life can be more frustrating than that of giving. For several years after I met Christ, I did not want to give and would always try to avoid it. On a few occasions, I found myself in a position in which I felt obligated to give in order to appear spiritual. I did so, but my heart wasn't in it.

My whole perspective changed after I learned what the Bible actually taught. I wanted to give; however, I was frustrated by another problem: an unlimited number of needs and my limited resources. How could I decide to whom to give? My church, the hungry poor, campus and prison ministries, missionary efforts, radio and television programs, and many other vital ministries needed financial support.

These decisions are even more difficult because of today's intense competition for a Christian's money. It seems as if my mailbox is constantly full of appeals. I react to these requests with mixed emotions: compassion, gratitude, despair, guilt, and even cynicism. I feel deep compassion when confronted with those facing starvation of body or spirit. I am grateful that there are people whose life purpose is to meet those needs. I almost despair at the unbelievable needs of those less fortunate than ourselves. I feel guilty that perhaps we are not giving enough. And I become cynical at being solicited for more and more money and perhaps being manipulated by people whose goals may be worthwhile but whose means of achieving those goals are questionable.

We will examine the four elements of giving: attitudes, advantages, amount, and approach.

ATTITUDES IN GIVING

God evaluates our actions on the basis of our attitudes. God's attitude toward giving is best summed up in John 3:16: *"For God so loved the world, that He gave His only begotten Son."* Note the sequence. Because God loved, He gave. Because God is love, He is also a giver. He set the example of giving motivated by love.

An attitude of love in giving is crucial: *"If I give all my possessions to feed the poor . . . but do not have love, it profits me nothing"* (1 Corinthians 13:3). It is difficult to imagine anything more commendable than giving everything to the poor. However, giving with the wrong attitude, without love, is of no benefit to the giver.

In God's economy the attitude is more important than the amount. Jesus

emphasized this in Matthew 23:23: *"Woe to you, teachers of the law and Pharisees, you hypocrites! You give a tenth of your spices—mint, dill and cummin. But you have neglected the more important matters of the law—justice, mercy and faithfulness. You should have practiced the latter without neglecting the former"* (NIV). The Pharisees had been careful to give the tithe (give 10 percent) —down to the last mint leaf in their gardens. However, Christ rebuked them because He looks past the amount of the gift to the heart of the giver.

The reason we can give out of a heart filled with love is that our gifts are actually given to the Lord Himself. An example of this is found in Numbers 18:24: *"The tithe of the sons of Israel . . . they offer as an offering to the Lord"* [emphasis mine]. If giving is merely to a church, a ministry, or a needy person, it is only charity. But if it is given to the Lord, it becomes an act of worship. Because God is our Creator, our Savior, and our faithful Provider, we can express our gratefulness and love by giving our gifts to Him.

For example, when the offering plate is being passed at church, we should remind ourselves that we are giving our gift to the Lord Himself.

In addition to giving out of a heart filled with love, we are to give cheerfully. *"Each one must do just as he has purposed in his heart, not grudgingly or under compulsion, for God loves a cheerful giver"* (2 Corinthians 9:7). The original Greek word for cheerful is *hilarios*, which is translated into the English word hilarious. We are to be hilarious givers.

Unfortunately, there is usually little hilarity in the pews when the offering plate is passed in church. In fact, the atmosphere more often reminds us of a patient waiting in the dentist chair who knows a painful extraction is about to occur.

How do we develop this hilarity in our giving? Consider the early churches of Macedonia.

> *"We want you to know about the grace that God has given the Macedonian churches. Out of the most severe trial, their overflowing joy and their extreme poverty welled up in rich generosity"* (2 Corinthians 8:1-2, NIV).

GIVING NOTES

How did the Macedonians, who were in terrible circumstances, *"severe trial"* and *"extreme poverty,"* still manage to give with *"overflowing joy"*? The answer is in verse 5: *"They gave themselves first to the Lord and then to us in keeping with God's will."* The key to cheerful giving is to submit ourselves to Christ and ask Him to direct how much He wants us to give. Only then are we in a position to experience any of the advantages by giving with the proper attitude.

Stop and examine yourself. What is your attitude toward giving?

ADVANTAGES OF GIVING

"What's this we hear about you laying up treasures in heaven?"

Obviously a gift benefits the recipient. The church continues its ministry, the hungry are fed, the naked are clothed and missionaries are sent. But, according to God's economy, a gift given with the proper attitude benefits the giver more than the receiver. *"Remember the words of the Lord Jesus, that He Himself said, 'It is more blessed to give than to receive'"* (Acts 20:35). As we examine Scripture, we find that the giver benefits in four significant areas.

1. Increase in Intimacy

Above all else, giving directs our attention and heart to Christ. Matthew 6:21 tells us, *"For where your treasure is, there your heart will be also."* This is why it is so necessary to give each gift to the person of Jesus Christ. When you give your gift to Him, your heart will automatically be drawn to the Lord.

Also remember that giving is one of the responsibilities of the steward, and the more faithful you are in fulfilling these responsibilities the more you can *"enter into the joy of your Master"* (Matthew 25:21). Nothing in life can compare to entering into His joy and knowing Christ more intimately.

2. Increase in Character

Our heavenly Father wants us as His children to be conformed to the image of His Son. The character of Christ is that of an unselfish giver. Unfortunately, humans are selfish by nature. One of the key ways we become conformed to Christ is by regular giving. Someone once said, "Giving is not God's way of raising money; it is God's way of raising people into the likeness of His Son."

3. Increase in Heaven

Matthew 6:20 reads, *"Store up for yourselves treasures in heaven, where neither moth nor rust destroys, and where thieves do not break in or steal."* The Lord tells us that there really is something akin to the "First National Bank of Heaven." He wants us to know that we can invest for eternity.

Paul wrote, *"Not that I seek the gift itself, but I seek for the profit which increases to your account"* (Philippians 4:17). There is an account for each of us in heaven that we will be able to enjoy for eternity. And although it is true

GIVING NOTES

that we "can't take it with us," Scripture teaches that we can make deposits to our heavenly account before we die.

4. Increase on Earth

Many people have a hard time believing that giving results in material blessings flowing back to the giver; however, study the following passages.

Proverbs 11:24-25 says, *"There is one who scatters, and yet increases all the more, and there is one who withholds what is justly due, and yet it results only in want. The generous man will be prosperous, and he who waters will himself be watered."*

Examine 2 Corinthians 9:6-11.

> *"He who sows sparingly will also reap sparingly, and he who sows bountifully will also reap bountifully. . . . God is able to make all grace abound to you, so that always having all sufficiency in everything, you may have an abundance for every good deed; as it is written, 'He scattered abroad, He gave to the poor, His righteousness endures forever.' Now He who supplies seed to the sower and bread for food will supply and multiply your seed for sowing and increase the harvest of your righteousness; you will be enriched in everything for all liberality."*

These verses clearly teach that giving results in a material increase: *"will also reap bountifully . . . always having all sufficiency in everything . . . may have an abundance . . . will supply and multiply your seed . . . you will be enriched in everything."*

But note carefully **why** the Lord is returning an increase materially: *"Always having all sufficiency in everything, you may have an abundance for every good deed . . . will supply and multiply your seed for sowing . . . you will be enriched in everything for all liberality."* As shown in the diagram below the Lord produces an increase so that we may give more and have our needs met at the same time.

Study the cycle in giving.

Give / Needs Met / Material Increase

One reason the Lord reveals that a gift will result in material increase is because He wants us to recognize that He is behind it. God has chosen to be invisible, but He wants us to experience His reality.

When we give, we should do so with a sense of anticipating the Lord to provide a material increase, even though we do not know when or how the Lord may choose to provide it. From our experience, He can be very creative! Remember, the giver can experience the advantages of giving only when he

When we give, we should do so with a sense of anticipating the Lord to provide a material increase, even though we do not know when or how the Lord may choose to provide it. From our experience, He can be very creative!

or she gives cheerfully out of a heart filled with love—not when the motive of giving is just to get.

AMOUNT TO GIVE

Let's survey what the Scripture says about how much to give. Before the Old Testament Law was given, there were two instances of giving with a known amount. In Genesis 14:20 Abraham gave 10 percent—a tithe—after the rescue of his nephew Lot. And in Genesis 28:22 Jacob promised to give the Lord a tenth of all his possessions if God brought him safely through his journey.

After the Law was given, a tithe was required. The Lord condemns the children of Israel in Malachi 3:8-9 for not tithing properly: *"Will a man rob God? Yet you are robbing Me! But you say, 'How have we robbed You?' In tithes and offerings. You are cursed with a curse, for you are robbing Me, the whole nation of you!"*

In addition to the tithe, there were various offerings. The Lord also made special provisions for the needs of the poor. Every seven years all debts were forgiven; every 50 years the land was returned to the original land-owning families. And there were special rules for harvesting that allowed the poor to glean behind the harvesters.

God made another significant provision for the poor in Deuteronomy 15:7-8: *"If there is a poor man with you, one of your brothers, in any of your towns in your land which the Lord your God is giving you, you shall not harden your heart, nor close your hand from your poor brother; but you shall freely open your hand to him, and shall generously lend him sufficient for his need in whatever he lacks."* Even under the law, the extent of one's giving was not limited by a fixed percentage but was in part dictated by the needs of the surrounding people.

The New Testament teaches that we are to give in proportion to the material blessing we receive. It also commends sacrificial giving.

What I like about the tithe is that it is systematic, and the amount of the gift is easy to compute. The danger of the tithe is that it can be treated as simply another bill to be paid, and by not having the correct attitude I do not put myself in a position to receive the blessings God has for me when I give. Another potential danger of tithing is the assumption that once I have tithed I have fulfilled all my obligations to give. For many Christians, the tithe should be the beginning of their giving, not the limit.

How much should we give? To answer this question, first give yourself to the Lord. Submit yourself to Him. Earnestly seek His will for you concerning giving. Ask Him to help you obey Christ's leading. We are convinced that we should tithe as a minimum and then give over and above the tithe as the Lord prospers or directs us.

During Paul's third missionary journey one of his priorities was to take up a collection for the suffering believers in Jerusalem. There are several practical applications from his instructions concerning this collection. *"On the first day of every week each one of you is to put aside and save, as he may prosper, so that no collections be made when I come"* (1 Corinthians 16:2).

1. Giving Should Be Periodic

"On the first day of every week." The Lord understands that we need to give frequently. Giving only once a year is a mistake. We need to give regularly to be drawn consistently to Christ.

2. Giving Should Be Personal

"Each one of you is to." It is the responsibility of every child of God, whether young or old, rich or poor, to give. The advantages of giving are intended for each person, and to be enjoyed each individual must participate.

3. Giving Should Be Out of a Private Deposit

"That was the best sermon on giving I've ever heard."

"Put aside and save." If you experience difficulty in monitoring the money you have decided to give, consider opening a separate account or setting aside a special "cookie jar" into which you deposit the money you intend to give. Then, as needs are brought to your attention, you already will have the money to meet those needs.

4. Giving Should Be a Priority

"Honor the Lord from your wealth and from the first of all your produce" (Proverbs 3:9). As soon as we receive any income, we should set aside the amount we are going to give. This habit helps us to remember to put Christ first in all we do and defeats the temptation to spend on ourselves the portion we have decided to give.

5. Giving Should Be Premeditated

"Each one must do just as he has purposed in his heart" (2 Corinthians 9:7). Our giving should be done prayerfully, exercising the same care in selecting where we are going to give our money as we do when deciding where to invest our money.

6. Giving Should Be Without Pride

To experience any of the Lord's benefits, your giving cannot be motivated out of a desire to impress people. Matthew 6:1-4 says, *"Be careful not to do your 'acts of righteousness' before men, to be seen by them. If you do, you will have no reward from your Father in heaven. So when you give to the needy, do not announce it with trumpets, as the hypocrites do in the synagogues and on the streets, to be honored by men. . . . They have received their reward in full. But when you give to the needy, do not let your left hand know what your right hand is doing, so that your giving may be in secret. Then your Father, who sees what is done in secret, will reward you"* (NIV).

GIVING NOTES

In Scripture we are instructed to give to three areas. To whom and in what proportion one gives varies with the needs God lays on the heart of each believer.

1. Giving to the Local Church and Christian Ministries

Throughout its pages the Bible focuses on funding the ministry. The Old Testament priesthood was to receive specific support: *"To the sons of Levi, behold, I have given all the tithe in Israel...in return for their service which they perform"* (Numbers 18:21). And the New Testament teaching on ministerial support is just as strong. Unfortunately, some have wrongly taught poverty for Christian workers. Thus many believe that those who are in Christian ministry should be poor. That position is not scriptural.

"Pastors who do their work well should be paid well and should be highly appreciated, especially those who work hard at both preaching and teaching" (1 Timothy 5:17, TLB).

How many Christian workers have been driven to distraction from their ministry by inadequate support? God never intended His servants to exist at the level of bare subsistence. As someone has said, "The poor and starving pastor should exist only among poor and starving people."

People ask us if we give only through our church. In our case, the answer is no. However, giving to the local church should be a priority. We do give a minimum of 10 percent of our regular income through our church, because this is a tangible expression of our commitment to our church. But we also give to others who are directly impacting us. *"The one who is taught the word is to share all good things with the one who teaches"* (Galatians 6:6).

"Hi, Pastor. We were just talking about your request for a salary increase."

2. Giving to the Poor

In Matthew 25:34-45 we are taught one of the most exciting and yet sobering truths in Scripture. Read this passage carefully.

"The King will say . . . 'For I was hungry and you gave Me something to eat; I was thirsty, and you gave Me something to drink.' . . . Then the righteous will answer Him, 'Lord, when did we see You hungry, and feed You, or thirsty, and give You something to drink?' . . . The King will answer and say to them, . . . 'To the extent that you did it to one of these brothers of Mine, even the least of them, you did it to Me.' Then He will also say to those on His left, 'Depart from Me, accursed ones, into the eternal fire . . . for I was hungry, and you gave Me nothing to eat; I was thirsty, and you gave Me nothing to drink. . . . To the extent that you did not do it to one of the least of these, you did not do it to Me.'"

In some mysterious way we cannot fully understand, Jesus, the Creator of all things, personally identifies Himself with the poor. When we share with

GIVING NOTES

the needy we are actually sharing with Jesus Himself. And if that truth is staggering, then this is terrifying—when we do not give to the needy, we leave Christ Himself hungry and thirsty.

During Christ's earthly ministry He gave consistently to the poor. When Jesus told Judas to go and carry out the betrayal during the Last Supper, *"no one of those reclining at the table knew for what purpose He had said this to him. For some were supposing, because Judas had the money box, that Jesus was saying to him, 'Buy things we have need of for the feast'; or else, that he should give something to the poor"* (John 13:28-29).

Giving to the needy was such a consistent part of Jesus' life that the disciples assumed that Jesus was sending Judas either to buy needed food or to give to the poor; no other alternative entered their minds.

After Paul met with the disciples to announce his ministry to the Gentiles, he said, *"They* [the disciples] *only asked us to remember the poor—the very thing I also was eager to do"* (Galatians 2:10). Imagine all the issues the disciples could have discussed with Paul, but the only one they mentioned was to remember the poor. Now that should tell us something!

There are three areas of our Christian lives that are affected by giving or lack of giving to the poor.

■ Prayer

A lack of giving to the poor could be a source of unanswered prayer. *"Is this not the fast which I choose . . . to divide your bread with the hungry and bring the homeless poor into the house? . . . Then you will call and the Lord will answer"* (Isaiah 58:6-9). *"He who shuts his ear to the cry of the poor will also cry himself and not be answered"* (Proverbs 21:13).

■ Provision

Our provision is partially conditioned upon our giving to the needy. *"He who gives to the poor will never want, but he who shuts his eyes will have many curses"* (Proverbs 28:27).

■ Knowing Jesus Christ intimately

One who does not share with the poor does not know the Lord as intimately as he or she could. *"'He pled the cause of the afflicted and the needy; then it was well. Is that not what it means to know Me?' declares the Lord"* (Jeremiah 22:16).

Giving to the poor has been discouraged, in part, because of government programs. We believe it's the church's job and not the government's to meet the needs of the poor. The government often treats the needy impersonally. The church has the potential to be sensitive to the dignity of the needy. We also can develop one-on-one relationships to meet their immediate physical needs and then focus on their longer-term physical and spiritual needs.

If you don't already know those who are needy, please consider asking the Lord to bring one needy person into your life. You can do so by praying this prayer: "Father God, by Your grace create in me the desire to share with the needy. Bring a poor person into my life so that I might learn what it really

> *When we share with the needy we are actually sharing with Jesus Himself.*

GIVING NOTES

means to give." This will be a significant step in your maturing in your relationship with Christ. Mother Theresa is probably the best example in our time of serving the poor in a loving, compassionate way.

May we be able to echo Job's statement: *"I delivered the poor who cried for help, and the orphan who had no helper. . . . I made the widow's heart sing for joy. . . . I was eyes to the blind and feet to the lame. I was a father to the needy, and I investigated the case which I did not know"* (Job 29:12-16).

Secular Charities

Numerous secular charities (such as schools, fraternal orders, or organizations that fight diseases) compete vigorously for our gift dollars. Scripture does not address whether we should give to these charities. However, our family has decided not to normally support these organizations with our gifts. Our reason is that even though many people support secular charities, only those who know the Lord support the ministries of Christ. However, we occasionally give to secular charities, either when the solicitor is a friend we want to encourage or influence for Christ or we sense the Lord's prompting to give.

Summary

Although the area of giving can be challenging, if done with the proper attitude it can become one of the most exciting and vibrant parts of your Christian experience.

GOING DEEPER

For more information on giving, we recommend the organization Generous Giving as an excellent resource. Please visit their Web site at **www.generousgiving.org**.

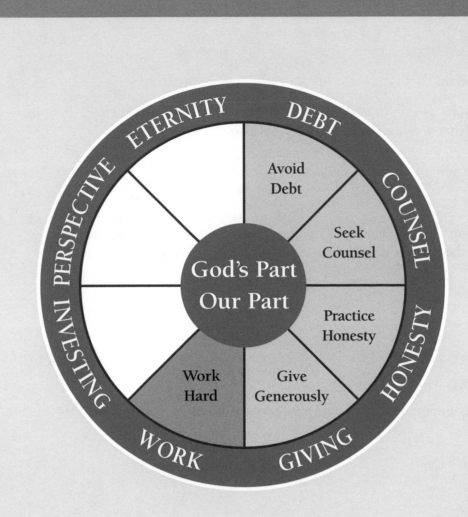

Work Diligently
As unto the Lord

"Whatever you do, do your work heartily, as for the Lord rather than for men. . . . It is the Lord Christ whom you serve"
(Colossians 3:23-24).

WORK ♛

Scripture to Memorize

"Whatever you do, do your work heartily, as for the Lord rather than for men. . . . It is the Lord Christ whom you serve" (Colossians 3:23-24).

Practical Application: ☐ Complete the Your Checking Account practical application. NOTE: Please give your leader the name of anyone who would be interested in becoming a student in a future group.

DAY ONE

Read the Giving Notes on pages 84 to 92.

1. From God's perspective, it is important to give with the proper attitude. How will this influence your giving?

2. What truth about giving did you learn that proved especially helpful? In what way?

Read *Genesis 2:15.*

1. Why is it important to recognize that the Lord created work before sin entered the world?

Read *Genesis 3:17-19.*

2. What was the consequence of sin on work?

Read *Exodus 20:9* and *2 Thessalonians 3:10-12.*

3. What do these passages say to you about work?

    Exodus 20:9—

    2 Thessalonians 3:10-12—

WORK

Read *Genesis 39:2-5; Exodus 35:30-35; Exodus 36:1-2;* **and** *Psalm 75:6-7.*

1. What do these verses tell us about the Lord's involvement in our work?

    Genesis 39:2-5—

    Exodus 35:30-35—

    Exodus 36:1-2—

    Psalm 75:6-7—

2. How do these truths differ from the way most people view work?

3. How will this perspective impact your work?

WORK

Read *Ephesians 6:5-9; Colossians 3:22-25;* and *1 Peter 2:18.*

1. What responsibilities do the employer and employee have according to these verses?

Employee responsibilities:

Employer responsibilities:

2. For whom do you really work? How will this understanding change your work performance?

DAY FIVE

Read *Proverbs 6:6-11; Proverbs 18:9;* and *2 Thessalonians 3:7-9.*

1. What does the Lord say about working hard?

Proverbs 6:6-11—

Proverbs 18:9—

2 Thessalonians 3:7-9—

2. Do you work hard? If not, describe what steps you will take to improve your work habits.

Read *Exodus 34:21.*

3. What does this verse communicate to you about rest?

4. Do you get enough rest?

5. How do you guard against overwork?

Read *Proverbs 31:10-28* **and** *Titus 2:4-5.*

1. What do these passages tell us about women working?

    Proverbs 31:10-28—

    Titus 2:4-5—

2. If you are a woman, how does this apply to your situation?

Read *2 Corinthians 6:14-18.*

3. How does this concept of "yoking" or "being bound together" apply to partnerships in business and work?

4. Can you give some examples from the Bible of people who retired?

5. Do you think retirement, as it is practiced in our culture, is biblically acceptable? Why or why not?

 Please write your prayer requests in your Prayer Log before coming to class.

 I will take the following action as a result of this week's study.

WORK NOTES

Please do not read these notes until you have completed the Work Homework.

Over a lifetime, the average person spends 100,000 hours working. But, often with the job comes some degree of dissatisfaction. Perhaps no statistic demonstrates this more than the changing of jobs. A survey found that the average man changes jobs every four and one-half years, the average woman every three years.

Boredom, lack of fulfillment, inadequate wages, and countless other pressures have contributed to this discontentment. Doctors, housewives, salespersons, bluecollar workers, and managers—regardless of the profession—all have experienced similar frustrations. Understanding scriptural principles that relate to work will help you find satisfaction in your job. It will also place you in a position in which the Lord can prosper you.

BIBLICAL PERSPECTIVE OF WORK

Even before sin entered the human race, God instituted work. *"The Lord God took the man and put him into the garden of Eden to cultivate it and keep it"* (Genesis 2:15). The very first thing the Lord did with Adam was to put him to work. Despite what many believe, work was initiated for our benefit in the sinless environment of the garden of Eden. Work is not a result of the curse!

After the fall, work was made more difficult.

> *"Cursed is the ground because of you; in toil you will eat of it all the days of your life. Both thorns and thistles it shall grow for you; and you will eat the plants of the field; by the sweat of your face you will eat bread"* (Genesis 3:17-19).

Work is so important that in Exodus 34:21 God gives this command: *"You shall work six days."* In the New Testament Paul is just as direct. *"If anyone is not willing to work, then he is not to eat"* (2 Thessalonians 3:10). Examine the verse carefully. It says, *"If anyone is not **willing** to work."* It did not say, *"If anyone cannot work."* This principle does not apply to those who are physically or mentally unable to work. It is for those who are able but choose not to work.

A close friend has a brother in his mid-thirties whose parents have always supported him. He has never had to face the responsibilities and hardships involved in a job. As a consequence, his character has not been properly developed. He is hopelessly immature in many areas of his life.

One of the primary purposes of work is to develop character. While the carpenter is building a house, the house is also building the carpenter. The carpenter's skill, diligence, manual dexterity, and judgment are refined. A job is

A job is not merely a task designed to earn money; it is also intended to produce godly character in the life of the worker.

not merely a task designed to earn money; it's also intended to produce godly character in the life of the worker.

ALL HONEST PROFESSIONS ARE HONORABLE

According to Scripture there is dignity in all types of work. Scripture does not elevate any honest profession above another. A wide variety of vocations are represented in the Bible. David was a shepherd and a king. Luke was a doctor. Lydia was a retailer who sold purple fabric. Daniel was a government worker. Paul was a tentmaker. And, finally, the Lord Jesus was a carpenter.

In God's economy there is equal dignity in the labor of the automobile mechanic and the president of General Motors, in the labor of the pastor and a secretary serving the church.

There is dignity in all types of work. Scripture does not elevate any honest profession above another.

GOD'S PART IN WORK

Scripture reveals three responsibilities the Lord has in work.

1. God Gives Job Skills

Exodus 36:1 illustrates this truth: *"Every skillful person in whom the Lord has put skill and understanding to know how to perform all the work . . . shall perform."* God has given each of us unique skills. People have a wide variety of abilities, manual skills, and intellectual capacities. It is not a matter of one person being better than another; it is simply a matter of having received different abilities.

2. God Gives Success

The life of Joseph is a perfect example of God helping a person to succeed. *"The Lord was with Joseph, so he became a successful man. . . . His master saw that the Lord was with him and how the Lord caused all that he did to prosper"* (Genesis 39:2-3). We have certain responsibilities, but it is ultimately God who gives success.

3. God Controls Promotion

Psalm 75:6-7 says, *"For promotion and power come from nowhere on earth, but only from God"* (TLB). As much as it may surprise you, our bosses are not the ones who control whether we will be promoted. Understanding this should have a tremendous impact on the way we perform as employees. Most people find this hard to believe. They leave God out of work and believe they alone are responsible for their job skills and control their success. However, those with a biblical understanding approach work differently.

One of the major reasons people experience stress and frustration in their jobs is because they don't understand God's part in work. Stop reading for a few minutes. Think about God's part—He gives you your skills and controls success and promotion. How should this perspective impact you and your job?

Scripture reveals we actually are serving the Lord in our work and not people. *"Whatever you do, do your work heartily, as for the Lord rather than for men. . . . It is the Lord Christ whom you serve"* (Colossians 3:23-24). Recognizing that we are really working for the Lord has profound implications.

Consider your attitude toward work. If you could see Jesus Christ as your boss, would you try to be more faithful in your job? The most important question you need to answer every day as you begin your work is this: "For whom do I work?" You work for Christ.

WORK HARD

"Whatever your hand finds to do, do it with all your might" (Ecclesiastes 9:10, NIV). *"The precious possession of a man is diligence"* (Proverbs 12:27). In Scripture hard work and diligence are encouraged; laziness is condemned: *"He who is slack in his work is brother to him who destroys"* (Proverbs 18:9).

Paul's life was an example of hard work.

> *"With labor and hardship we kept working night and day so that we might not be a burden to any of you . . . in order to offer ourselves as a model for you, so that you might follow our example"* (2 Thessalonians 3:8-9).

"SO MR. PHELPS, WHAT MAKES YOU THINK THAT YOU'RE EXPERIENCING BURNOUT?"

Your work should be at such a level that people will never equate laziness with God. Nothing less than hard work and the pursuit of excellence pleases the Lord. We are not required to be "superworkers" who never make mistakes. Rather, the Lord expects us to do the best we possibly can.

BUT DO NOT OVERWORK!

Hard work, however, must be balanced by the other priorities of life. If your job demands so much of your time and energy that you neglect your relationship with Christ or your loved ones, then you are working too hard. You should determine whether the job is too demanding or your work habits need changing. If you tend to be a "workaholic," be careful that you don't forsake the other priorities of life.

Exodus 34:21 reads, *"You shall work six days, but on the seventh day you shall rest; even during plowing time and harvest you shall rest."* We believe this Old Testament principle of resting one day out of seven has application today. This has been difficult for me, particularly during times of "plowing or harvesting," when a project deadline is approaching or I am under financial pressure.

Rest can become an issue of faith. Is the Lord able to make our six days of work more productive than seven days? Yes! The Lord instituted weekly rest for our physical, mental, and spiritual health. Study the following diagram to understand the balance God wants in our lives.

WORK NOTES

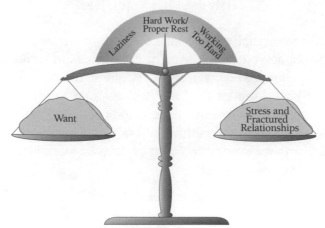

A Balanced Life with Contentment

EMPLOYER'S RESPONSIBILITIES

The godly employer performs a balancing act. The employer is to love, serve, and encourage employees. Yet, the employer also is responsible to lead employees and to hold them accountable for the completion of their assigned tasks. Let's examine several principles that should govern an employer's conduct.

1. Serve Your Employees

The basis for biblical leadership is servanthood: *"Whoever wishes to become great among you shall be your servant"* (Matthew 20:26). Too often employers have concentrated on producing a profit at the expense of their personnel. However, the Bible directs the employer to balance efforts to make a profit with an unselfish concern for employees. Employees are to be treated fairly and with genuine dignity. *"Masters [employers], grant to your slaves [employees] justice and fairness, knowing that you too have a Master in heaven"* (Colossians 4:1).

Employers should attempt to be creative as they serve their employees. For example, they should consider investing time and money to educate and upgrade their employees' job skills. This will help employees grow in their capabilities and thus earn more.

2. Be a Good Communicator

The Genesis account of building the tower of Babel supports the importance of good communication. At that time, everyone spoke the same language and adopted a common goal. The Lord makes this remarkable observation, *"If as one people speaking the same language they have begun to do this, then nothing they plan to do will be impossible for them"* (Genesis 11:6, NIV).

When a group of people are committed to accomplishing a particular task and there is good communication, then *"nothing they plan to do will be impossible for them"*—as long as it's within the will of God. Since building the tower was not what He wanted, He stopped construction. He disrupted their ability to communicate, which was the foundation for successfully completing the tower. *"Come, let us go down and confuse their language so they will not understand each other"* (Genesis 11:7, NIV).

When a group of people are committed to accomplishing a particular task and there is good communication, then "nothing they plan to do will be impossible for them"—as long as it's within the will of God.

It's especially important to listen to employee complaints. *"If I have despised the claim of my . . . [employees] when they filed a complaint against me, what then could I do when God arises? And when He calls me to account, what will I answer Him?"* (Job 31:13-15). A sensitive, listening ear is a tangible expression that you care about the other person. When a complaint is legitimate, the employer should take appropriate steps to solve the problem.

3. Hold Employees Accountable

The employer is responsible for the employees knowing what is expected on the job. The employer should regularly evaluate employee performance and communicate this to them. If an employee is not performing satisfactorily and is unable or unwilling to change, it may necessitate a personnel change.

4. Pay Your Employees a Fair Wage Promptly

Employers are warned to pay a fair wage. "[The Lord will judge] *those who oppress the wage earner in his wages*" (Malachi 3:5). They also are commanded to pay wages promptly when due. *"You shall not oppress a hired [employee]. . . . Give him his wages on his day before the sun sets . . . so that he will not cry against you to the Lord and it become sin"* (Deuteronomy 24:14-15).

5. Pray for Godly Employees

The Lord may choose to bless an employer for having a godly employee. Scripture gives two examples of this. First of all, *"Laban said to [Jacob], 'If I have found favor in your eyes, please stay; . . . the Lord has blessed me because of you'"* (Genesis 30:27, NIV). Secondly, *"Joseph found favor in [Potiphar's] sight. . . . It came about that from the time he made [Joseph] overseer in his house and over all that he owned, the Lord blessed the Egyptian's house on account of Joseph; thus the Lord's blessing was upon all that he owned, in the house and in the field"* (Genesis 39:4-5).

Because of this principle I wanted to employ Raymond who was an especially godly construction worker. He was strong and did the work of two people. But far more important was Raymond's influence over the project. There was less profanity and pilferage, and he was an excellent model to everyone. This principle is not a command, but we believe the wise employer will pray for the Lord to bring a "Raymond" to his or her company.

EMPLOYEE'S RESPONSIBILITIES

We can identify the six major responsibilities of the godly employee by examining the story of Daniel in the lion's den. In Daniel chapter 6 we are told that Darius, the king of Babylon, appointed 120 people to administer the government and three people, one of whom was Daniel, to supervise the administrators. King Darius decided to promote Daniel to govern the entire kingdom. Daniel's fellow employees then looked for a way to remove him from his job. After this failed they asked King Darius to enact a law that required everyone to worship only the king or else die in the lion's den. Daniel was thrown to the lions after refusing to stop worshipping the Lord.

A sensitive, listening ear is a tangible expression that you care about the other person. When a complaint is legitimate, the employer should take appropriate steps to solve the problem.

God then rescued Daniel by sending an angel to shut the lions' mouths. The following are six characteristics of a godly employee.

1. Honesty

Daniel 6:4 tells us that Daniel's fellow employees could find no dishonesty in him, and there was no *"evidence of corruption"* in his work. Daniel was totally honest. We studied the importance of honesty earlier.

2. Faithfulness

We discover the second characteristic of a godly employee in Daniel 6:4: *"He was faithful."* The godly employee needs to establish the goal of being faithful and excellent in work, then to work hard to reach that goal.

3. Prayerfulness

The godly employee is a person of prayer. *"When Daniel knew that the document was signed* [restricting worship to the king alone] *. . . he continued kneeling on his knees three times a day, praying and giving thanks before his God, as he had been doing previously"* (Daniel 6:10). Daniel's job was that of governing the most powerful country of his day. Few of us will ever be faced with Daniel's responsibilities and the demands upon his time. Yet he knew the importance of prayer. If you are not praying consistently, your work is suffering.

4. Honors Employer

"Daniel spoke to the king, 'O king, live forever!'" (Daniel 6:21). What a remarkable response from Daniel. The king had been tricked into sentencing Daniel to the lion's den. But Daniel's reaction was to honor his employer. Think how natural it would have been to say something like, "You dummy! The God who sent His angel to shut the lions' mouths is now going to punish you!" Instead, he honored his employer.

The godly employee always honors his or her superior. *"Servants* [employees], *be submissive to your masters* [employers] *with all respect, not only to those who are good and gentle, but also to those who are unreasonable"* (1 Peter 2:18). One way to honor your employer is to never gossip behind your employer's back, even if he or she is not an ideal person.

5. Honors Fellow Employees

People may damage your reputation to secure a promotion over you or even have you fired from your job. They tried to murder Daniel. Despite this, there is no evidence that Daniel did anything but honor his fellow employees. *"Do not slander a servant* [employee] *to his master* [employer], *or he will curse you"* (Proverbs 30:10, NIV).

The godly person should avoid office politics and manipulation to secure a promotion. Your boss does not control your promotion; the Lord Himself does. We can be content in our jobs by trying to be faithful, honoring superiors, and encouraging other employees. Having done this, we can rest, knowing that Christ will promote us if and when He chooses.

The godly employee always honors his or her superior. "Servants [employees] be submissive to your masters [employers] with all respect, not only to those who are good and gentle, but also to those who are unreasonable" (1 Peter 2:18).

6. Verbalizes Faith

King Darius would never have known about the Lord if Daniel had not communicated his faith at appropriate moments while at work. *"The king spoke and said to Daniel, 'Daniel, servant of the living God, has your God, whom you constantly serve, been able to deliver you from the lions?'"* (Daniel 6:20). King Darius would not have been as powerfully influenced by Daniel sharing his faith if he had not observed his honesty, faithfulness, and hard work. Listen to the words of Darius: *"I issue a decree that in every part of my kingdom people must fear and reverence the God of Daniel. For He is the living God and He endures forever"* (Daniel 6:26, NIV).

Daniel influenced his employer, one of the most powerful people in the world, to believe in the only true God. You have that same opportunity in your own God-given sphere of work. Let me say this another way. A job well done earns you the right to tell others with whom you work about the reality of Christ. As we view our work from God's perspective, dissatisfaction will turn to contentment from a job well done, and drudgery will become excitement over the prospect of introducing others to the Savior.

OTHER WORK ISSUES

RETIREMENT

The dictionary defines retirement as: "withdrawal from an occupation, to retreat from an active life." The goal of retirement is deeply ingrained in our culture. Many people retire and cease all labor to live a life filled with leisure.

Numbers 8:24-26 is the only reference to retirement in Scripture. The instruction there applied only to the Levites who worked on the tabernacle. As long as one is physically and mentally capable, there is no scriptural basis for a person retiring and becoming unproductive. The concept of putting an older but able person "out to pasture" is unbiblical. Age is no obstacle in finishing the work the Lord has for you to accomplish. He will provide you with the necessary strength. For example, Moses was 80 years old when he began his 40-year adventure of leading the children of Israel.

FROM THE WALL STREET JOURNAL—PERMISSION, CARTOON FEATURES SYNDICATE

"I can't retire! I haven't paid off my student loan yet."

Scripture does imply that the type or the intensity of work may change as we grow older—a shifting of the gears to a less demanding pace to become more of an "elder seated at the gate." During this season of life we can use the experience and wisdom gained over a lifetime. If we have sufficient income to meet our needs apart from our jobs, we may choose to leave work to invest more time in serving others in whatever way the Lord directs.

AMBITION

Scripture does not condemn ambition. Paul was ambitious. *"We also have as our ambition . . . to be pleasing to Him"* (2 Corinthians 5:9). However, our ambition should not be selfish. The Lord *"will render to each person according to his deeds . . . to those who are selfishly ambitious . . . wrath and indignation"* (Romans 2:6,8). *"But if you have . . . selfish ambition in your heart, do not be arrogant and so lie against the truth. This wisdom is not that which comes down from above, but is earthly, natural, demonic. For where . . . selfish ambition exist, there is disorder and every evil thing"* (James 3:14-16). *"But you, are you seeking great things for yourself? Do not seek them"* (Jeremiah 45:5).

The Bible is not the enemy of ambition, only of the wrong type of ambition. The motivation for our ambition should be to please Christ. We should desire to become an increasingly faithful steward in using the possessions and skills God has given us. In our work we should try to please the Lord by doing our jobs to the best of our abilities.

> *The Bible is not the enemy of ambition, only of the wrong kind of ambition.*

YOUR CALLING

Each of us has a specific calling or purpose that the Lord intends for us. *"We are His workmanship, created in Christ Jesus for good works, which God prepared beforehand so that we would walk in them"* (Ephesians 2:10). Study this passage carefully. *"We are His workmanship."* The Amplified Bible says, *"We are His handiwork."* Each of us has been given special physical, emotional, and mental abilities. You may have heard the expression, "After the Lord made you, He threw away the mold!" It's true! You are gifted uniquely. No one in all of history—past, present or future—is like you.

The passage continues, *"created in Christ Jesus for good works, which God prepared beforehand so that we would walk in them."* The Lord created each of us for a particular job, and He endowed us with the skills and desires to accomplish this work. This calling may be full-time Christian service or a secular job. Often people struggle with whether God wants them to continue in their work after they commit their lives to Christ. Many feel they are not serving Christ in a significant way if they remain at their jobs. Nothing could be further from the truth. The key is for each person to determine God's call for his or her life.

In his book, *God Owns My Business*, Stanley Tamm writes, "Although I believe in the application of good principles in business, I place far more confidence in the conviction that I have a call from God. I am convinced that His purpose for me is in the business world. My business is my pulpit." To those who earn a living through secular pursuits, it is a great comfort to know that the "call" of holy vocation carries over into all walks of life. God strategically places His children everywhere!

PARTNERSHIPS

Scripture discourages business partnerships with those who do not know Christ. In 2 Corinthians 6:14-17 we read, *"Do not be bound together with unbelievers;*

for what partnership have righteousness and lawlessness, or what fellowship has light with darkness? . . . or what has a believer in common with an unbeliever? . . . 'Therefore, come out from their midst and be separate, says the Lord.'" Many have violated this principle and have suffered financially.

In our opinion, we should also be careful before entering into a partnership even with another Christian. I would consider only a few people as partners. These are people I know well. I have observed their commitment to the Lord. I know their strengths and weaknesses and have seen them handle money faithfully. **Do not rush into a partnership!**

Before forming a partnership, reduce your understandings into writing. Develop this agreement with your future partner, and be sure to include a way to end the partnership. If you are not able to agree in writing, do not become partners.

PROCRASTINATION

A procrastinator is someone who, because of laziness or fear, has a habit of putting things off until later. Often this habit can develop into a serious character flaw.

The Bible has many examples of godly people who were not procrastinators, and one of my favorite examples is Boaz. Naomi, the mother-in-law of Ruth, made this comment about Ruth's future husband Boaz: *"Wait, my daughter, until you know how the matter turns out; for the man will not rest until he has settled it today"* (Ruth 3:18). Boaz had the reputation of a person who acted promptly.

FRANK'S NOT WHAT YOU'D CALL A MORNING PERSON.

Here are some practical suggestions to help overcome procrastination: (1) List the things you need to do each day. (2) Prayerfully review the list and prioritize it according to the tasks you need to accomplish first. (3) Finish the first task on your list before starting the second. Often that first task is the most difficult or the one you fear the most. (4) Ask the Lord to give you courage, remembering Philippians 4:13, *"I can do all things through Him who strengthens me."*

WIVES WORKING OUTSIDE THE HOME

For many reasons, women work in jobs of all kinds. Married women work to provide additional income for their families, to express their creativity, or because they enjoy their jobs. Single women work to provide their needs.

In our opinion, during the children's early formative years, if possible, it is preferable for the mother to be home when the children are home, unless the family finances depend upon her income. Titus 2:4-5 reads, *"Encourage the young women to love their husbands, to love their children, to be sensible, pure, workers at home."* As the children mature, a mother will have increased freedom to pursue outside work.

Proverbs 31:10-31 reads, *"An excellent wife . . . does him [her husband] good and not evil all the days of her life. She looks for wool and flax and works with her hands. . . . She brings her food from afar. She rises also while it is still night*

Couples often are surprised to learn that the income earned by a second working spouse is not as much as they had expected.

and gives food to her household. . . . She considers a field and buys it; from her earnings she plants a vineyard. . . . She stretches out her hands to the distaff, and her hands grasp the spindle. She extends her hand to the poor. . . . She makes coverings for herself; her clothing is fine linen and purple. Her husband is known in the gates, when he sits among the elders of the land. She makes linen garments and sells them, and supplies belts to the tradesmen. . . . She looks well to the ways of her household, and does not eat the bread of idleness."

Proverbs 31 paints a picture of the working wife living a balanced life with the thrust of her activity toward the home. Some women are gifted as homemakers, and there is no more important task than raising godly children. However, other women must work to earn income, or they have the skill and desire to work outside the home. Either way, it is a decision that the married couple should make together.

TWO-INCOME FAMILIES

If both the husband and wife work outside the home, it is helpful to determine what income, after taxes and expenses, the second wage contributes. In the "Example 1" column of the worksheet on the next page, the following assumptions have been made, based on working 40 hours a week and earning $9 per hour; giving 10 percent of the gross income; federal income tax of 25 percent (a second income is added to the first and taxed at the higher rate); state income tax of 5 percent; Social Security tax of 7.5 percent; 10 trips of five miles at a cost of 25 cents a mile; lunch, snacks, and coffee breaks of $15; eating out more often and using convenience foods add $35 a week to the budget; $20 for extra clothing and cleaning is needed; $5 more is spent for grooming; extra child care of $45 a week. In the "Example 2" column we assume earning $25 an hour, with all other assumptions remaining the same.

These assumptions are for illustration only and may not represent your situation. Complete the exercise on the following page to determine the actual income after expenses.

Couples often are surprised to learn that the income earned by a second working spouse is not as much as they had expected. Some have actually produced more net income (after reducing work-related expenses) when they decided to work in some creative way while staying at home. Of course, the financial benefits are not the only factors to evaluate. Consideration also should be given to the physical and emotional demands of working and how they affect a family.

Income and Spending for Second Wage Earner	Example 1	Example 2	Your Situation
Gross yearly income:	$ 18,720.00	$ 52,000.00	
Gross weekly income:	$ 360.00	$ 1,000.00	
Expenses:			
Giving	$ 36.00	$ 100.00	
Federal income tax	$ 90.00	$ 250.00	
State income tax	$ 18.00	$ 50.00	
Social Security tax	$ 27.00	$ 75.00	
Transportation	$ 15.00	$ 15.00	
Lunch/snacks/coffee breaks	$ 15.00	$ 15.00	
Restaurants/convenience food	$ 35.00	$ 35.00	
Extra clothing/cleaning	$ 20.00	$ 20.00	
Personal grooming	$ 5.00	$ 5.00	
Child care	$ 45.00	$ 45.00	
TOTAL EXPENSES:	$ 306.00	$ 610.00	
NET ADDITIONAL FAMILY INCOME:	$ 54.00	$ 390.00	
NET INCOME PER HOUR:	$ 1.35	$ 9.75	

GOING DEEPER

For further study about biblical principles for running a business, we recommend Larry Burkett's *Business by the Book*. Also, be sure to visit the Web site of Fellowship of Companies for Christ at **www.christianity.com/fcci** for resources, advice, and encouragement on how you can develop a ministry within your company.

WORK NOTES

Consistently Save

"Steady plodding brings prosperity"
(Proverbs 21:5, TLB).

Scripture to Memorize

"Steady plodding brings prosperity; hasty speculation brings poverty"
(Proverbs 21:5, TLB).

Practical Application: ☐ Complete the "Organizing Your Estate" practical application and continue your budget. ☐ Remember to secure a current will if you do not yet have one.

DAY ONE

Read the Work Notes on pages 101 to 111.

1. What in the notes proved especially helpful or challenging? How will this impact you?

2. Do you usually recognize you are working for the Lord? If not, what can you do to be more aware that you work for the Lord?

Read *Genesis 41:34-36; Proverbs 21:20;* and *Proverbs 30:24-25*.

1. What do these passages say to you about savings?

    Genesis 41:34-36—

    Proverbs 21:20—

    Proverbs 30:24-25—

2. If you are not yet saving, how do you propose to begin?

Read *Luke 12:16-21,34*.

3. Why did the Lord call the rich man a fool?

4. According to this parable, why do you think it is scripturally permissible to save only when you are also giving?

Read *1 Timothy 5:8.*

1. What is a scripturally acceptable goal for saving?

Read *1 Timothy 6:9.*

2. What is a scripturally unacceptable reason for saving?

Read *1 Timothy 6:10.*

3. According to this verse, why is it wrong to want to get rich (refer to *1 Timothy 6:9*)? Do you have the desire to get rich?

Read *1 Timothy 6:11.*

4. What should you do if you have the desire to get rich?

INVESTING

Read *Proverbs 21:5; Proverbs 24:27; Proverbs 27:23-24; Ecclesiastes 3:1; Ecclesiastes 11:2;* and *Isaiah 48:17-18.*

1. What investment principle(s) can you learn from each of these verses, and how will you apply each principle to your life?

Proverbs 21:5—

Proverbs 24:27—

Proverbs 27:23-24—

Ecclesiastes 3:1—

Ecclesiastes 11:2—

Isaiah 48:17-18—

Read *Genesis 24:35-36; Proverbs 13:22;* and *2 Corinthians 12:14.*

1. Should parents attempt to leave a material inheritance to their children?

2. How are you going to implement this principle?

Read *Proverbs 20:21* and *Galatians 4:1-2.*

3. What caution should a parent exercise?

    Proverbs 20:21—

    Galatians 4:1-2—

Gambling is defined as: *playing games of chance for money and betting*. Some of today's most common forms of gambling are casino wagering, betting on sporting events, horse and dog races, and state-run lotteries.

1. What are some of the motivations that cause people to gamble?

2. Do these motives please the Lord? Why?

Read *Proverbs 28:20* **and** *Proverbs 28:22*.

3. According to these passages, why do you think a godly person should not gamble (play lotteries, bet on sporting events)?

4. How does gambling contradict the scriptural principles of working diligently and being a faithful steward of the Lord's possessions?

 Please write your prayer requests in your Prayer Log before coming to class.

 I will take the following action as a result of this week's study.

We must answer a question before we can say investing is scripturally legitimate. Is money evil? The answer to that is a resounding "No"! Money can be used for good or evil, for supporting missionaries and building hospitals, or for financing hard drugs and pornography. The Bible never condemns money itself, only the misuse of or the wrong attitude toward it.

LEGITIMATE INVESTING

Examine 1Timothy 6:10 carefully: *"The love of money is a root of all sorts of evil."* Not the money itself, but the wrong attitude toward money is the root of much evil. Particularly in the Old Testament, many of the most godly people were also among the more wealthy people of the day. Job, Abraham, and David were all wealthy, and yet they did not allow wealth to interfere with their relationship with the Lord.

> *The Bible never condemns money itself, only the misuse of or the wrong attitude toward it.*

It seems difficult to explain Matthew 6:19-21, which seems to speak against saving and investing: *"Do not store up for yourselves treasures on earth, where moth and rust destroy, and where thieves break in and steal. But store up for yourselves treasures in heaven . . . for where your treasure is, there your heart will be also."*

Jesus clarifies this issue in the parable of a rich man who laid up treasures for himself. *"The land of a rich man was very productive. And he began reasoning to himself, saying, 'What shall I do, since I have no place to store my crops?' Then he said, 'This is what I will do: I will tear down my barns and build larger ones, and there I will store all my grain and my goods. And I will say to my soul, "Soul, you have many goods laid up for many years to come; take your ease, eat, drink and be merry." But God said to him, 'You fool! This very night your soul is required of you; and now who will own what you have prepared?' So is the man who lays up treasures for himself, and is not rich toward God. . . . For where your treasure is, there your heart will be also"* (Luke 12:16-21, 34).

The key word in this parable is "all." Jesus called the rich man a fool because he saved **all** of his goods. He stored them up for his own use. He did not balance his saving with generous giving. We should save and invest only when we also are giving to the Lord. Why? *"Where your treasure is, there your heart will be also"* (Matthew 6:21). If we concentrate solely on saving and investing, our focus and affection will gravitate to those possessions. But if we balance our saving and investing by giving generously to the Lord, we can still love Christ first with all our hearts.

INVESTMENT GOALS

Before you develop your individual investment strategy, you must establish investment goals. We believe three goals are acceptable for investing.

1. To Provide for You and Your Family

In 1 Timothy 5:8 we read, *"If anyone does not provide for his own, and especially for those of his household, he has denied the faith and is worse than an unbeliever."* This principle extends to providing for your needs in old age and leaving an inheritance to any children you may have.

2. To Become Free Financially to Serve the Lord

One objective of saving is to reduce our dependence on a salary to meet our needs. This affords us the freedom to invest more volunteer time in ministry if this is God's plan for us. The more income our savings and investments produce, the less we are dependent on income from our job. Some have saved enough to be free one day a week, and others are in a position to be full-time volunteers without the need to earn salaries.

3. To Operate Your Business

Another purpose for saving and investing is to accumulate enough capital to open and operate a business without going into debt. The amount of money will vary substantially, depending on the requirements of each business.

HOW MUCH IS ENOUGH?

When a runner breaks the tape at the finish line, he or she rarely continues running. However, some people who already have achieved the three acceptable investment goals continue accumulating. We believe that each of us should establish a maximum amount we are going to accumulate, and once we have "finished this race," we should give away the portion of our income that we were saving. This "finish line" on accumulation protects us against the dangers of hoarding.

UNACCEPTABLE INVESTMENT GOALS

One investment goal—the desire to become rich—is prohibited. First Timothy 6:9 states, *"Those who want to get rich fall into temptation and a snare and many foolish and harmful desires which plunge men into ruin and destruction."* Study this carefully. It does not say most of those who want to get rich; it says those who want to get rich. **Everyone** who wants to get rich will *"fall into temptation and a snare and many foolish and harmful desires which plunge men into ruin and destruction."*

Nothing is wrong with becoming wealthy if it is a by-product of being a faithful steward.

For most of my life I wanted to become rich—not just a little rich—enormously rich! So dealing with the biblical prohibition against this attitude has been painful. Sometimes, even now, I vacillate between wanting to get rich and wanting to be a faithful steward. When I want to get rich, I am self-centered. My motivations for wanting to get rich may vary: pride, greed, or an unhealthy desire to prepare for survival in an uncertain economic future. But when I want to be a faithful steward, I am Christ-centered in my thoughts and attitudes. My actions are then motivated by a pure heart. I am serving Christ and growing closer to Him.

The next verse, 1 Timothy 6:10, reveals another reason our Lord warns us not to want to get rich: *"For the love of money is a root of all sorts of evil, and some by longing for it have wandered away from the faith and pierced themselves with many griefs."* When we want to get rich, Scripture tells us that we are loving money

> *"No one can serve two masters. Either he will hate the one and love the other, or he will be devoted to the one and despise the other. You cannot serve both God and Money"* (Matthew 6:24, NIV).

When we want to get rich, we are actually loving money and hating God. We are devoted to money and despising God. First Timothy 6:10 ends by saying, *"Some by longing for riches have wandered away from the faith and pierced themselves with many griefs."* I have witnessed this firsthand. I admired and respected the man who led me to Christ. However, he became consumed by a desire to get rich. He divorced his wife and abandoned his four young sons. He denied Christ repeatedly and left the faith. Wanting to get rich, which is the love of money, is a devastating spiritual condition.

Understand me clearly. I am not saying it is wrong to become rich. In fact, I rejoice seeing God enable a person to prosper who has been ambitious enough to be a faithful steward. **Nothing is wrong with becoming wealthy if it is a by-product of being a faithful steward.**

THE TEMPTATION TO BECOME RICH

How can we overcome the temptation to get rich? By remembering to split and submit! In the next verse, 1 Timothy 6:11, Paul counsels Timothy to *"flee from these things* [the desire to get rich], *you man of God, and pursue righteousness, godliness, faith, love, perseverance and gentleness."* When you become aware of your desire to become rich, you must run from that temptation and replace it with the pursuit of godliness. Analyze what triggers your desire. I discovered an unrecognized habit of dreaming about becoming rich whenever I would take a long automobile trip alone. I started to break the habit by listening to Christian music to help me concentrate on the Lord while I was driving.

Secondly, the ultimate way of escape is found in submitting to Jesus as Lord. We can do this in perfect confidence because Jesus overcame a massive temptation to become rich. After Christ fasted 40 days in the wilderness, the devil tempted Him three times. The final temptation is recorded in Luke 4:5-7: *"He [the devil] led Him [Jesus] up and showed Him all the kingdoms of the world in a moment of time. And the devil said to Him, 'I will give You all this domain and its glory . . . if You worship before me.'"*

Jesus was exposed to all the kingdoms of the world in an instant of time. But because He was submitted entirely to the Father and empowered by the same Holy Spirit who lives in us, He was able to resist that temptation.

We are of the opinion that our heavenly Father usually will not allow His children to prosper when they are motivated to get rich. Wanting to get rich—loving money—closely parallels greed. And *"greed . . . amounts to idolatry"* (Colossians 3:5). The Father watches closely over His children to ensure that we will not be drawn away from loving Him with all of our hearts.

SAVING

Once we have established our investment goals, the first step is saving. Unfortunately, most people are not consistent savers. The average person in our country is three weeks away from bankruptcy with little or no money saved, significant debt, and is totally dependent on next week's paycheck to keep the budget afloat.

Scripture encourages us to save. *"The wise man saves for the future, but the foolish man spends whatever he gets"* (Proverbs 21:20, TLB). The ant is commended for saving for a future need. *"Four things on earth are small, yet they are extremely wise: ants are creatures of little strength, yet they store up their food in the summer"* (Proverbs 30:24-25, NIV). Having savings is the opposite of being in debt. Saving is making **provision** for tomorrow, but debt is **presumption** upon tomorrow.

We call saving the "Joseph principle," because saving requires self-denial. Joseph saved during seven years of plenty to survive during seven years of famine. Saving is denying an expenditure today so that you will have something to spend in the future. One of the major reasons most people are poor savers is that the average person does not practice self-denial. When we want something, we want it now!

HOW TO SAVE AND HOW MUCH TO SAVE

The most effective way to save is to do it every time you receive income. The first check you write should be your gift to the Lord, and the second check you write should go to your savings. An automatic payroll deduction can help ensure that a portion of your income is saved regularly. Some save income from tax refunds or bonuses. Remember that if you immediately save a portion of your income each time you are paid, you will save more. The Bible does not teach a percentage to be saved. We recommend establishing a goal of saving 10 percent of your income. This may not be possible initially, but begin the habit of saving—even if it's only a dollar a month.

THERE ARE TWO TYPES OF SAVINGS

1. Long-Term Savings

Long-term savings are intended to fund long-term needs and goals, such as retirement income. Pensions and retirement accounts fall into this category. Except for extreme emergencies, these savings should not be used for any other purpose. They could be called "never-to-spend savings."

2. Short-Term Savings

Short-term savings should be in an account that is easily accessible, which may include interest-bearing accounts, mutual funds, and so forth. These are designed to be used for planned future spending: buying or replacing items such as appliances or cars and making major home repairs. Short-term savings should also be set aside for emergencies: an illness, loss of job, or other interruption of income. Financial experts recommend you save the equivalent of three to six months of income for this fund.

INVESTING

People place some of their savings in investments in the hope of receiving an income or growth in value. **The purpose of this** CROWN FINANCIAL MINISTRIES **study is not to recommend any specific investments. No one is authorized to use affiliation with** CROWN **to promote the sale of any investments or financial services.** Our objective is to draw attention to the scriptural framework for savings and investing. Visit CROWN's Web site for more detailed information on investing.

STEADY PLODDING

"Steady plodding brings prosperity; hasty speculation brings poverty" (Proverbs 21:5, TLB). The original Hebrew words for *"steady plodding"* picture a person filling a large barrel one handful at a time. Little by little the barrel is filled to overflowing.

The fundamental principle you need to practice to become a successful investor is to spend less than you earn. Then save and invest the difference over a long period of time.

Examine various investments. Almost all of them are well suited for "steady plodding." A home mortgage is paid off after years of steady payments. Savings grow because of compounding interest, and a business can increase steadily in value through the years as its potential is developed.

The fundamental principle you need to practice to become a successful investor is to spend less than you earn. Then save and invest the difference over a long period of time.

UNDERSTANDING COMPOUND INTEREST

A wealthy man was asked if he had seen the seven wonders of the world. He responded, "No, but I do know the eighth wonder of the world—compound interest." Understanding how compounding works is very important. There are three variables in compounding: the amount you save, the percentage rate you earn, and the length of time you save.

1. The Amount

The amount you save will be determined by your income and how much you spend for your living expenses, giving, and debt. It is our hope that you will increase the amount available for saving as you apply these biblical principles.

2. Rate of Return

The second variable is the rate you earn on an investment. The following table demonstrates how an investment of $1,000 a year grows at various rates.

Percent Earned	Year 5	Year 10	Year 20	Year 30	Year 40
6%	5,975	13,972	38,993	83,802	164,048
8%	6,336	15,645	49,423	122,346	279,781
10%	6,716	17,531	63,003	180,943	486,851
12%	7,115	19,655	80,699	270,293	859,142

As you can see, the increase in the rate has a remarkable effect on the amount accumulated. A 2 percent increase almost doubles the amount over 40 years. However, be careful not to make investments that are too risky in order to achieve a high return. Usually the higher the rate, the higher the risk.

3. Time

Time is the third factor. Answer this question: Who do you think would accumulate more by age 65, a person who started to save $1,000 a year at age 21, saved for eight years, and then completely stopped, or a person who saved $1,000 a year for 37 years who started at age 29? Both earned 10 percent. Is it the person who saved a total of $8,000 or the one who saved $37,000? Study the following chart.

INDIVIDUAL A			INDIVIDUAL B		
Age	Contribution	Year-End Value	Age	Contribution	Year-End Value
21	$1,000	$1,100	21	0	0
22	1,000	2,310	22	0	0
23	1,000	3,641	23	0	0
24	1,000	5,105	24	0	0
25	1,000	6,716	25	0	0
26	1,000	8,487	26	0	0
27	1,000	10,436	27	0	0
28	1,000	12,579	28	0	0
29	0	13,837	29	$1,000	$1,100
30	0	15,221	30	1,000	2,310
31	0	16,743	31	1,000	3,641
32	0	18,417	32	1,000	5,105
33	0	20,259	33	1,000	6,716
34	0	22,284	34	1,000	8,487
35	0	24,513	35	1,000	10,436
36	0	26,964	36	1,000	12,579
37	0	29,661	37	1,000	14,937
38	0	32,627	38	1,000	17,531
39	0	35,889	39	1,000	20,384
40	0	39,478	40	1,000	23,523
41	0	43,426	41	1,000	26,975
42	0	47,769	42	1,000	30,772
43	0	52,546	43	1,000	34,950
44	0	57,800	44	1,000	39,545
45	0	63,580	45	1,000	44,599
46	0	69,938	46	1,000	50,159
47	0	76,932	47	1,000	56,275
48	0	84,625	48	1,000	63,003
49	0	93,088	49	1,000	70,403
50	0	103,397	50	1,000	78,543
51	0	112,636	51	1,000	87,497
52	0	123,898	52	1,000	97,347
53	0	136,290	53	1,000	108,182
54	0	149,919	54	1,000	120,100
55	0	164,911	55	1,000	133,210
56	0	181,402	56	1,000	147,631
57	0	199,542	57	1,000	163,494
58	0	219,496	58	1,000	180,943
59	0	241,446	59	1,000	200,138
60	0	265,590	60	1,000	221,252
61	0	292,149	61	1,000	244,477
62	0	321,364	62	1,000	270,024
63	0	353,501	63	1,000	298,127
64	0	388,851	64	1,000	329,039
65	0	**$427,736**	65	$1,000	**$363,043**

Total Investment **$8,000**   **Total Investment** **$37,000**

Incredibly, the person who saved only $8,000 accumulated more because that person started saving earlier. The moral of this illustration: Start saving now.

This graph may help you better visualize the benefits of starting now. If a person faithfully saves $2.74 each day—$1,000 a year—and earns 10 percent, at the end of 40 years the savings will grow to $486,852 and will be earning $4,057 each month. Steady plodding pays.

However, if the person waits one year before starting, then saves for 39 years, $45,260 less will be accumulated. Start saving today!

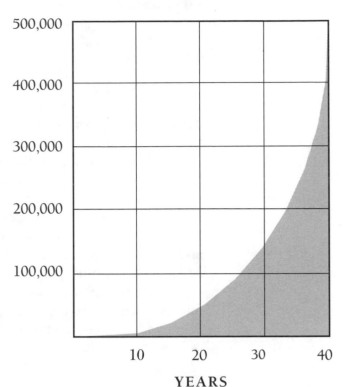

YEARS
$1,000 invested each year, earning 10%

AVOID RISKY INVESTMENTS

"There is another serious problem I have seen everywhere—savings are put into risky investments that turn sour, and soon there is nothing left to pass on to one's son. The man who speculates is soon back to where he began—with nothing" (Ecclesiastes 5:13-15, TLB).

Scripture warns of avoiding risky investments, yet each year thousands of people lose money in highly speculative and sometimes fraudulent investments. How many times have you heard of people losing their life's savings on some get-rich-quick scheme? Sadly, it seems that Christians are particularly vulnerable to such schemes, because they trust others who appear to live by the same values they do. We have known of investment scandals in churches, where "wolves in sheep's clothing fleeced the flock." Below are three characteristics that will help you identify a risky investment.

1. An unusually high profit or interest rate that is "practically guaranteed."
2. The decision to invest must be made quickly. There will be no opportunity to investigate the investment or promoter who is selling the investment. The promoter often will be doing you a "favor" by allowing you to invest.
3. Little will be said about the risks of losing money, and the investment usually will require no effort on your part. Sometimes a portion of the profits are said to be "dedicated to the Lord's work."

Before participating in any investment, please be patient and do your homework.

DIVERSIFY

> *"Divide your portion to seven, or even to eight, for you do not know what misfortune may occur on the earth"* (Ecclesiastes 11:2).

No investment on this earth is guaranteed. Money can be lost on any investment. The government can make gold illegal. The value of real estate can decrease. Money can be inflated until it is valueless. The stock market can perform well or crash.

My father's friend, Mr. Russell, was very successful in the stock market. When I was young he used to advise me, "When you grow up, invest in the stock market. It's the one sure way to become financially independent." When I was 25, I met Mr. Russell again. The stock market was in the midst of a significant decline. He said, "I've done a great deal of research on the stock market and the *Titanic*. Do you know the only difference between the two? The *Titanic* had a musical band!"

The perfect investment does not exist. We need to diversify. Consider the following steps as you diversify. I recommend that you not skip any of the steps. Begin with step one, and then take each step at a time.

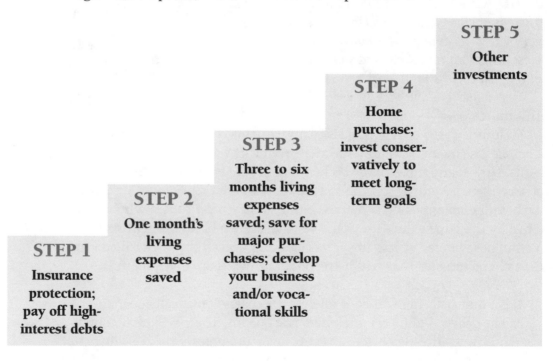

STEP 1
Insurance protection; pay off high-interest debts

STEP 2
One month's living expenses saved

STEP 3
Three to six months living expenses saved; save for major purchases; develop your business and/or vocational skills

STEP 4
Home purchase; invest conservatively to meet long-term goals

STEP 5
Other investments

COUNTING THE COST

With every investment there are costs: financial costs, time commitments, efforts required, and sometimes even emotional stress. For example, the purchase of a rental house will require time and effort to rent and maintain. If the tenant is irresponsible, you may have to try to collect rent from someone who does not want to pay—talk about emotions! Before you decide on any investment, carefully consider all the costs.

TIMING

> *"There is an appointed time for everything. And there is a time*
> *for every event under heaven"* (Ecclesiastes 3:1).

The right investment at the wrong time is the wrong investment. The decision to purchase or sell an investment is best made prayerfully after seeking counsel.

OTHER ISSUES

Gambling and Lotteries

Lotteries and gambling of all types are sweeping our country. A recent study discovered that people spend 15 times more money on gambling than they donate to churches! The average church member gives $20 a year to international missions, and the average person gambles $1,174 annually.

Sadly, millions of compulsive gamblers regularly lose their incomes. Their stories are heartbreaking. The Bible does not specifically prohibit gambling. However, many gamble in an attempt to **get rich quick.** This is a violation of Scripture.

In our opinion, a godly person should *never* participate in gambling or lotteries—even for entertainment. We should not expose ourselves to the risk of becoming compulsive gamblers; nor should we support an industry that enslaves so many.

Inheritance

Parents should attempt to leave an inheritance to their children. *"A good man leaves an inheritance to his children's children"* (Proverbs 13:22). The inheritance should not be dispensed until the child has been trained to be a wise steward. *"An inheritance gained hurriedly at the beginning will not be blessed in the end"* (Proverbs 20:21). In our opinion, you should provide in your will for distributing an inheritance over several years or until heirs are mature enough to handle the responsibility of money. Select those you trust to supervise youths until they are capable stewards.

> *"As long as the heir is a child, he does not differ at all from a slave*
> *although he is owner of everything, but he is under guardians and*
> *managers until the date set by the father"* (Galatians 4:1-2).

Wills

It is important to prepare financially for your death. As Isaiah told Hezekiah, *"Thus says the Lord, 'Set your house in order, for you shall die'"* (2 Kings 20:1). Someday, if the Lord does not first return you will die. One of the greatest gifts you can leave your loved ones for that emotional time will be an organized estate and a properly prepared will or revocable living trust. If you do not have a current will or trust, please make an appointment this week with an attorney to prepare one.

In our opinion, a godly person should never participate in gambling or lotteries—even for entertainment. We should not expose ourselves to the risk of becoming compulsive gamblers; nor should we support an industry that enslaves so many.

INVESTING NOTES

God loves us deeply. Consider what Jesus said in John 15:9, *"Just as the Father has loved me, I have also loved you."* Imagine the depth of love God the Father has for God the Son. In the same way, He loves you! And just as a loving earthly father desires a close relationship with his children, so our heavenly Father hungers for such a relationship with each of us.

God understands human nature perfectly and the particular challenge that wealth presents as a potential barrier to this intimate relationship with Him. If you have a measure of wealth, the Lord is not disappointed or surprised; rather, He intentionally entrusted it to you for a purpose. In 1 Timothy 6:17-19, the Lord issues a set of instructions designed to help those with resources to remain undistracted from loving Him.

1. Do Not Be Conceited

"Instruct those who are rich in this present world not to be conceited" (1 Timothy 6:17). Wealth tends to produce pride. For several years we drove two vehicles. The first was an old pickup truck that cost $100. It looked as if it cost $100! When I drove that truck to the bank drive-in window to cash a check, I was humble. I knew the cashier was going to carefully check my account to confirm that the driver of that beat-up truck had sufficient funds in his account. I was so patient! And when I received the money, I was so grateful. I drove away with a song in my heart and praises on my lips.

Our other vehicle was a well-preserved, second-hand automobile that was expensive when it was new. When I drove that car to the bank, I appeared to be a different person. I was a person of means who deserved a certain amount of respect. I was not quite as patient when the cashier examined my account, and when I received the money I was not as grateful. Wealth often leads to conceit.

James 1:9-10 addresses this issue: *"The brother of humble circumstances is to glory in his high position; and the rich man is to glory in his humiliation, because like flowering grass he will pass away."* The poor should be encouraged as children of the King of kings, while the rich are to remain humble, because life is short. If you have been entrusted with some wealth, remain humble before the Lord and other people.

2. Put No Confidence in Your Assets

> *"Instruct those who are rich in this present world not . . . to fix their hope on the uncertainty of riches, but on God, who richly supplies us with all things to enjoy"* (1 Timothy 6:17).

This is a struggle for many. It is easy to trust in money, because money can buy things. We tend to trust in the seen rather than in the invisible living God. We need to remind ourselves that possessions can be lost and that the Lord alone can be fully trusted.

3. Give Generously

"Instruct them to do good, to be rich in good works, to be generous and ready to share, storing up for themselves the treasure of a good foundation for the future,

---

If you have a measure of wealth, the Lord is not disappointed or surprised; rather, He intentionally entrusted it to you for a purpose.

INVESTING NOTES

so that they may take hold of that which is life indeed" (1 Timothy 6:18-19). The Lord commands the wealthy to be generous and tells them of two benefits of their giving: (1) eternal treasures that they will enjoy in the future, and (2) the blessing of *"taking hold of that which is life indeed."* By exercising generosity they can live the fulfilling life God intends for them.

THE ONE GUARANTEED INVESTMENT

I was 28 years old when I was exposed to the only guaranteed investment. I started attending a weekly breakfast with several young businessmen and was impressed because they were smart and energetic. But, more than that, I was attracted to the quality of their lives. I did not know what they owned, but whatever it was I wanted it.

At that time I was part owner of a successful business, had married my wonderful wife, and lived in a comfortable home. I had everything I thought would bring me happiness and a sense of accomplishment, but I had neither. Something was missing.

I was surprised to hear these men speak openly of faith in God. I grew up going to church regularly, but it meant nothing to me. A friend described how I could enter into a personal relationship with Jesus Christ. He told me five biblical truths I had never understood before.

1. *God Loves You and Wants You to Know Him and Experience a Meaningful Life*

God created people in His own image, and He desires a close relationship with each of us. *"For God so loved the world, that He gave His only begotten Son, that whoever believes in Him shall not perish, but have eternal life"* (John 3:16). *"I [Jesus] came that they might have life, and have it abundantly"* (John 10:10).

When my son Matthew was in the first grade, he wanted to win the 100-yard dash at his school's field day. That was all he talked about for two months, but there was a problem. His classmate Bobby Dike was faster.

Field day finally arrived. They ran the 50-yard dash first, and Bobby beat Matthew badly. I will never forget when Matthew came up to me with tears in his eyes, pleading, "Daddy, please pray for me in the 100-yard dash. I've just got to win." My heart sank as I nodded.

With the sound of the gun, Matthew got off to a quick start. Halfway through the race he pulled away from the rest of his classmates and won. I lost control of myself! I was jumping and shouting! I had never before experienced such exhilaration. Then it occurred to me how much I loved my son. Although I love other people, I do not love them enough to give my son to die for them. But that is how much God the Father loved you. He gave His only Son, Jesus Christ, to die for you.

God created people in His own image, and He desires a close relationship with each of us.

2. Unfortunately, We Are Separated from God

God is holy—which means God is perfect, and He cannot have a relationship with anyone who is not perfect. My friend asked if I had ever sinned—done anything that would disqualify me as perfect. "Many times," I admitted. He explained that every person had sinned, and the consequence of sin was separation from God. *"All have sinned and fall short of the glory of God"* (Romans 3:23). *"Your sins have cut you off from God"* (Isaiah 59:2, TLB).

This diagram illustrates our separation from God. An enormous gap separates us from God. Individuals try without success to bridge this gap through their own efforts, such as philosophy, religion, or living a good moral life.

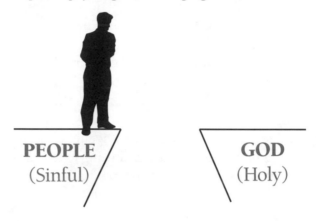

PEOPLE
(Sinful)

GOD
(Holy)

3. God's Only Provision to Bridge This Gap Is Jesus Christ

Jesus Christ died on the cross to pay the penalty for our sin. He bridged the gap between us and God. Jesus said, *"I am the way, and the truth, and the life; no one comes to the Father but through Me"* (John 14:6). *"God demonstrates His own love towards us, in that while we were yet sinners, Christ died for us"* (Romans 5:8).

This diagram illustrates our union with God through Jesus Christ.

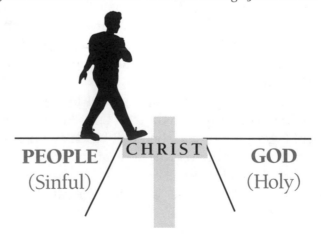

PEOPLE
(Sinful)

CHRIST

GOD
(Holy)

4. This Relationship Is a Gift from God

My friend explained that by an act of faith I could receive the free gift of a relationship with God. The transaction appeared unfair. In business, any time you had two people who were convinced they were getting more than they were giving up, you had a transaction. But now I was being offered a relationship with God, and it was a free gift!

> *"It is by grace you have been saved, through faith—this is not from yourselves, it is the gift of God—not by works, so that no one can boast"* (Ephesians 2:8-9, NIV).

5. We Must Each Receive Jesus Christ Individually

I had only to ask Jesus Christ to come into my life to be my Savior and Lord. And I did it. As my friends will tell you, I am a very practical person—if something does not work, I stop doing it quickly. I can tell you from 30 years experience that a relationship with the living God is available to you through Jesus Christ. Nothing compares with the privilege of knowing Christ personally. We can experience true peace, joy, and hope when we know Him.

If you desire to know the Lord and are not certain whether you have this relationship, I encourage you to receive Christ right now. Pray a prayer similar to this suggested one: "Father God, I need You. I invite Jesus to come into my life as my Savior and Lord and to make me the person You want me to be. Thank You for forgiving my sins and for giving me the gift of eternal life."

You might fulfill each of the principles in becoming a faithful steward, but without a relationship with Christ your efforts will be in vain. If you ask Christ into your life, please tell your small group leaders so they will be able to assist you in your spiritual growth.

You might fulfill each of the principles in becoming a faithful steward but, without a relationship with Christ, your efforts will be in vain.

INVESTING NOTES

"I have learned to be content in whatever circumstances I am. I know how to get along with humble means, and I also know how to live in prosperity. . . . I can do all things through Him who strengthens me"

(Philippians 4:11-13).

PERSPECTIVE HOMEWORK

 Scripture to Memorize

"I have learned to be content in whatever circumstances I am. I know how to get along with humble means, and I also know how to live in prosperity. . . . I can do all things through Him who strengthens me" (Philippians 4:11-13).

 Practical Application: ☐ Complete the Organizing Your Insurance practical application.

> Note: Think about your prayer request for the last class. It should be a "long-term" request the others can pray when they think of you.

DAY ONE

Read the Investing Notes on pages 120 to 133.

1. What in the notes proved especially helpful?

2. Carefully study the principle of compounding in the Investing Notes. Assume you earned 10 percent and saved $1,000 a year. Approximately how much would you accumulate by age 65 if you started saving today?

   $_____ *(refer to the graph on page 127 in the Investing Notes).*

3. Describe the specific steps you intend to take to begin saving.

Read *Deuteronomy 30:15-16; Joshua 1:8;* and *Hebrews 11:36-40*.

1. What do each of these passages communicate to you about financial prosperity for the believer?

   Deuteronomy 30:15-16—

   Joshua 1:8—

   Hebrews 11:36-40—

Reflect on the lives of Job, Joseph, and Paul.

2. Did they ever experience periods of financial abundance and at other times a lack of financial prosperity?

3. Was their lack of financial prosperity a result of sin or lack of faith?

4. Should all Christians always prosper financially? Why?

Read *Psalm 73:1-20*.

5. What does this passage tell you about the prosperity of the wicked?

P E R S P E C T I V E

Read *Philippians 4:11-13 and 1 Timothy 6:6-8.*

1. What do these passages say about contentment?

    Philippians 4:11-13 —

    1 Timothy 6:6-8 —

2. How does our culture discourage contentment?

3. How do you propose to practice contentment?

DAY FOUR

Read *Matthew 22:17-21 and Romans 13:1-7.*

1. Does the Lord require us to pay taxes to the government? Why?

Read *James 2:1-9.*

2. What does Scripture say about partiality (showing favoritism)?

3. Are you guilty of partiality based on a person's financial, educational, or social status?

Read *Romans 12:16* **and** *Philippians 2:3*.

4. How do you plan to overcome partiality?

DAY FIVE

Read Acts 4:32-37 and 1 Thessalonians 4:11-12.

1. What do these passages communicate to you about lifestyle?

    Acts 4:32-37—

    1 Thessalonians 4:11-12—

2. How do the following factors influence your present spending and lifestyle?
   - Comparing your lifestyle with that of friends and other people —

   - Television, magazines, catalogs, and other advertisements —

   - Your study of the Bible —

   - Your commitment to Christ and to things that are important to Him —

3. Do you sense that the Lord would have you change your spending or your standard of living? If so, in what way?

DAY SIX

Read *Deuteronomy 6:6-7; Proverbs 22:6;* **and** *Ephesians 6:4.*

1. According to these passages, who is responsible for teaching children how to handle money from a biblical perspective?

2. Stop and reflect for a few minutes: Describe how well you were prepared to manage money when you first left home as a young person?

3. Describe how you would train children to

   ▪ Budget –

   ▪ Give –

   ▪ Save –

   ▪ Spend wisely –

 Please write your prayer requests in your Prayer Log before coming to class.

 I will take the following action as a result of this week's study.

PERSPECTIVE NOTES

Please do not read these notes until you have completed the Perspective Homework.

In this chapter we will explore the Lord's perspective on a variety of issues: determining lifestyle, understanding prosperity, paying taxes, and teaching children about money.

LIFESTYLE

The Bible does not require one standard of living for everyone. In Scripture, godly people are represented in all walks of life, and the Lord still places His people in every level of society—rich and poor. We encourage you to evaluate your standard of living. To help you, examine several principles that should influence your lifestyle.

1. Learn to Be Content

The apostle Paul wrote in 1 Timothy 6:8: *"If we have food and covering* [clothes and shelter], *with these we shall be content."* If this were an advertisement, it would read something like this, "If you can afford the finest food, wear the latest fashions, and live in a beautiful home, then you will be happy." Our society operates on the assumptions that more is always better and that happiness is based on acquiring.

The word "contentment" is mentioned seven times in Scripture, and six times it has to do with money. Paul wrote, *"I have learned to be content in whatever circumstances I am. I know how to get along with humble means, and I also know how to live in prosperity; in any and every circumstance I have learned the secret of being filled and going hungry, both of having abundance and suffering need. I can do all things through Him who strengthens me"* (Philippians 4:11-13). Paul "learned" to be content. We are not born content; rather, we learn contentment.

There are three elements to the secret of contentment, as illustrated in the diagram below.

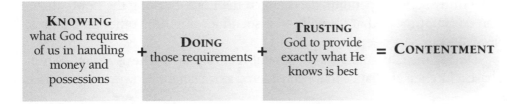

KNOWING what God requires of us in handling money and possessions **+** **DOING** those requirements **+** **TRUSTING** God to provide exactly what He knows is best **=** **CONTENTMENT**

Note carefully that it is not just knowing these things that brings contentment; it is doing them. Once we have been faithful in the doing, we can be content in knowing that our loving, heavenly Father will entrust the possessions He knows will be best for us at any particular time—whether much or little. Biblical contentment is not to be equated with laziness. Because we serve the living and dynamic God, Christians should always seek to improve. Contentment does not exclude properly motivated ambition. In fact, we should desire to be increasingly faithful stewards of the talents and possessions entrusted to us.

Biblical contentment is an inner peace that accepts what God has chosen for our present vocation and financial situation.

> *"Make sure that your character is free from the love of money, being content with what you have; for He Himself has said, 'I will never desert you, nor will I ever forsake you'"* (Hebrews 13:5).

2. Learn to Avoid Coveting

Coveting means to crave another's property, and it is prohibited throughout Scripture. The last of the Ten Commandments is, *"You shall not covet your neighbor's house; you shall not covet your neighbor's wife or his male servant or his female servant or his ox or his donkey or anything that belongs to your neighbor"* (Exodus 20:17). Note the broad application: *"anything that belongs to your neighbor."* In other words, we are commanded not to covet anything that belongs to anyone!

Greed is similar to coveting. *"Do not let immorality or any impurity or greed even be named among you. . . . For this you know with certainty, that no immoral or impure person or covetous man, who is an idolater, has an inheritance in the kingdom of Christ and God"* (Ephesians 5:3, 5).

A greedy or covetous person is an idolater. Coveting and greed have been called the silent sins. Rarely are they confronted, but they are among the most common of sins. When I began studying what the Bible taught about money, I was overwhelmed by the extent of my own coveting. Ask the Lord to show you if you are guilty of coveting something that is another's. If so, ask the Lord to change your heart.

3. Do Not Determine Your Lifestyle By Comparing It to Others

Some use comparison to justify spending more than they should. Many have suffered financially because they tried but could not afford to "keep up with the Joneses." Someone once said, "You can never keep up with the Joneses. Just about the time you've caught them, they go deeper in debt to buy more things!"

4. Freely Enjoy Whatever You Spend in the "Spirit"

Prayerfully submit spending decisions to the Lord. Seeking the Lord's direction does not mean that we will never spend for anything other than a basic necessity.

During the Christmas season several years ago, my wife asked me to purchase a kitchen appliance that I considered extravagant. However, I promised

The word "contentment" is mentioned seven times in Scripture, and six times it has to do with money.

to seek the Lord's direction. As we prayed, He made it clear that we should purchase the appliance, which we have thoroughly enjoyed. *"Everything created by God is good, and nothing is to be rejected if it is received with gratitude"* (1 Timothy 4:4).

5. Make an Effort to Live More Simply

Every possession requires time, and often money, to maintain. Too many or the wrong types of possessions can demand so much time or money that they harm our relationships with the Lord and others. A quiet, simple life is the safest environment for us to be able to invest enough time to nurture our relationships.

> *"Make it your ambition to lead a quiet life and attend to your own business and work with your hands, just as we commanded you, so that you will behave properly toward outsiders and not be in any need"* (1 Thessalonians 4:11-12).

Do not become unduly encumbered with the cares of this life. *"Suffer hardship with me, as a good soldier of Christ Jesus. No soldier in active service entangles himself in the affairs of everyday life, so that he may please the one who enlisted him as a soldier"* (2 Timothy 2:3-4).

6. Success Is Meaningless Apart from Serving Jesus Christ

King Solomon, the author of Ecclesiastes, had an annual income of more than $35 million. He lived in a palace that took 13 years to build. He owned 40,000 stalls of horses. The daily menu of his household included 100 sheep and 30 oxen.

Obviously, Solomon was in a position to know whether money would bring true fulfillment. He concluded, *"Vanity of vanities...all is vanity!"* (Ecclesiastes 12:8). Nothing, even extraordinary success, can replace the value of our relationship with the Lord. Ask yourself this question: Am I sacrificing a close relationship with Christ in the pursuit of wealth? *"What does it profit a man to gain the whole world, and forfeit his soul?"* (Mark 8:36).

7. Do Not Be Conformed to This World

Romans 12:2 says, *"Do not be conformed to this world."* The Amplified Bible says it this way: *"Do not be conformed to this world (this age), [fashioned after and adapted to its external, superficial customs]"* (Romans 12:2). We live in one of the most affluent cultures the world has ever known. We are constantly bombarded with advertising to prompt us to spend money. Advertisers usually stress the importance of image rather than function. For example, automobile ads rarely focus on a car as reliable transportation. Instead, they project an image of status or sex appeal.

No matter what the product—clothing, deodorants, credit cards, or anything else—the message is clear: the

"My problem has been that every time prosperity was just around the corner, so was the shopping center."

PERSPECTIVE NOTES

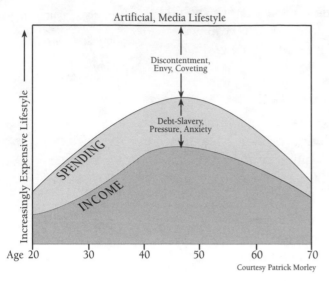

Artificial, Media Lifestyle

Discontentment,
Envy, Coveting

Debt-Slavery,
Pressure, Anxiety

SPENDING

INCOME

Increasingly Expensive Lifestyle

Age 20   30   40   50   60   70

Courtesy Patrick Morley

happy, beautiful, wrinkle-free life can be ours if we are willing to buy it. Unfortunately, to some extent this has influenced us all. Author George Fooshee states it so well, "People buy things they do not need with money they do not have to impress people they do not even like."

This graph depicts how the artificial, media-generated lifestyle influences our lives. The bottom curve represents our income—what we can afford to buy. The next curve illustrates what we actually spend. We make up the difference between our income and spending by the use of debt, which creates stress. The top of the graph demonstrates what advertisers tell us to buy. It is an expensive lifestyle that claims to satisfy our deepest needs. When we want to live this counterfeit dream but cannot afford it, we suffer discontentment.

From time to time we all get hooked on something we think we must buy. Once hooked, it is easy to rationalize a purchase of anything. Remember to seek the Lord's guidance and godly counsel when making a spending decision.

POVERTY, PROSPERITY, OR STEWARDSHIP?

Many Christians embrace one of two extremes about finances. On one hand, some believe that you must be poor, because a wealthy person cannot have a close relationship with Christ. However, the Bible does not say that a godly person must live in poverty. A number of godly people in Scripture were among the wealthiest individuals of their day. In the Old Testament the Lord extended the reward of abundance for obedience, but the threat of poverty was one of the consequences of disobedience.

> "I have set before you today life and prosperity, and death and adversity; in that I command you today to love the Lord your God, to walk in His ways and to keep His commandments . . . that the Lord your God may bless you" (Deuteronomy 30:15-16).

Psalm 35:27 says, "The Lord . . . delights in the prosperity of His servant." We may pray for prosperity when our relationships with the Lord are healthy and we have a proper perspective of possessions. "Beloved, I pray that in all respects you may prosper and be in good health, just as your soul prospers" (3 John 2).

On the other hand, some believe that all Christians who truly have faith will always prosper. This extreme is also in error. Study the life of Joseph. He is an example of a faithful person who experienced prosperity and poverty. He was born into a prosperous family, then was sold into slavery by his jealous brothers. While Joseph was a slave, his master promoted him to be head of his household. Later he made the right choice, not to commit adultery with his master's wife, yet he was thrown in jail for years because of that decision. In God's timing, he was ultimately elevated to prime minister of Egypt.

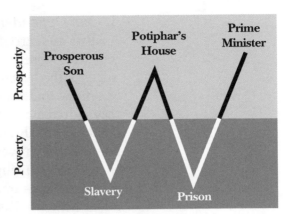

The guideline for prosperity is found in Joshua 1:8, *"This book of the law shall not depart from your mouth, but you shall meditate on it day and night, so that you may be careful to do according to all that is written in it; for then you will make your way prosperous, and then you will have success."*

Two requirements for prosperity become apparent from studying this passage. You must meditate on the Scriptures and engrave them on your mind and heart; and you are required to do all that is written in them. Once you have fulfilled these obligations, you place yourself in the position to be blessed financially, but there is no guarantee that the godly will always experience prosperity. There are four reasons the godly may not prosper.

1. Violating Scriptural Principles

Look again at Joshua 1:8. There is the requirement to do *all* that is written in the Bible. A person may be giving generously but acting dishonestly. A person may be honest but not fulfilling work responsibilities. A person may be a faithful employee but head-over-heels in debt. A person may be completely out of debt but not giving. One of the benefits of this study is that we explore what the entire Bible teaches about money. Those who do not understand all the requirements often neglect areas of responsibility unknowingly and suffer financially.

2. Building Godly Character

In Romans 5:3-4 we read, *"Tribulation brings about perseverance; and perseverance, proven character."* Many godly people in the Bible lived righteously, yet they lost their possessions. David became a national hero after slaying Goliath, only to be forced to flee for his life from a tormented King Saul. Job lost his children and possessions in the space of a few moments and was described as a *"blameless and upright man, fearing God and turning away from evil"* (Job 1:8). Paul learned the secret of contentment while being held captive in chains and suffering want, even though he was righteous.

God sometimes molds our character by allowing us to experience difficult circumstances. An example of how the Lord develops character in a people before prospering them is found in Deuteronomy 8:16-18: *"In the wilderness He fed you manna which your fathers did not know, that He might humble you and that He might test you, to do good for you in the end. Otherwise, you may say in your heart, 'My power and the strength of my hand made me this wealth.' But you shall remember the Lord your God, for it is He who is giving you power to make wealth."* Our Father knows us better than we know ourselves. In His infinite wisdom He knows exactly how much He can entrust to us at any time without it harming us.

3. Our Dependence and His Discipline

A father was carrying his two-year-old daughter as he waded in a lake. When they were close to shore, the child was unconcerned because of the apparent safety of the beach, even though the water was deep enough to drown her. She didn't understand her dependence upon her father. However, the farther they moved away from shore, the tighter the child held to her father. Like the child, we are always completely dependent upon the Lord to provide for us. However, often we don't recognize our dependence when we are "close to shore" experiencing the apparent security of financial prosperity. But when our possessions are few or none, it is easier to recognize our need and to cling to our heavenly Father.

And Hebrews 12:6,10 tells us that *"The Lord disciplines those he loves . . . for our good, so that we may share in his holiness"* (NIV). If we have sin in our lives or a wrong attitude toward money, out of the Lord's great love for us He may discipline us by allowing financial difficulties to encourage us to forsake our sin.

4. The Mystery of God's Sovereignty

In Hebrews 11 we find "Faith's Hall of Fame." In verses 1-35 we have a list of people who triumphed miraculously by the exercise of their faith in God. But in verse 36 the writer directs our attention to godly people who gained God's approval, yet experienced poverty. God ultimately chooses how much to entrust to each person, and sometimes we simply can't understand His decisions.

LET'S SUMMARIZE: The Scriptures teach neither the necessity of poverty nor uninterrupted prosperity. What the Bible teaches is the responsibility of being a faithful steward. Please review this chart which contrasts the three perspectives.

	Poverty	**Stewardship**	**Prosperity**
Possessions are	Evil	A responsibility	A right
I work to	Meet only basic needs	Serve Christ	Become rich
Godly people are	Poor	Faithful	Wealthy
Ungodly people are	Wealthy	Unfaithful	Poor
I give	Because I must	Because I love God	To get
My spending is	Without gratitude to God	Prayerful and responsible	Carefree and consumptive

It is important to understand the Lord's perspective of prosperity. The Lord evaluates true riches based on His spiritual value system, which is stated most clearly in Revelation. The godly poor are rich in God's sight. *"I [the Lord] know*

If we have sin in our lives or a wrong attitude toward money, the Lord may discipline us by allowing financial difficulties to encourage us to forsake our sin.

your tribulation and your poverty (but you are rich)" (Revelation 2:9). Those who are wealthy, yet do not enjoy a close relationship with Christ are actually poor. *"You say, 'I am rich, and have become wealthy, and have need of nothing,' and you do not know that you are wretched and miserable and poor and blind and naked"* (Revelation 3:17). True prosperity extends far beyond material possessions. True prosperity is gauged by how well we know Jesus Christ and by how closely we follow Him.

DANGERS OF PROSPERITY

Remember that God loves you deeply and He wants to enjoy a close relationship with you. Because of His love, the Lord reveals dangers associated with money that can pose a threat to our relationship with Him and other people. First, wealth tends to separate people. Abram and Lot were relatives. Their prosperity ultimately caused them to move away from each other. *"Abram was very rich in livestock, in silver and in gold. . . . [Lot] also had flocks and herds and tents. And the land could not sustain them while dwelling together, for their possessions were so great that they were not able to remain together"* (Genesis 13:2, 5-7). You probably know friends or family who have allowed conflicts over money to damage their relationships.

Second, it is easy for those who are prosperous to turn from God. *"When I [the Lord] bring them into the land . . . and they have eaten and are satisfied and become prosperous, then they will turn to other gods and serve them, and spurn Me"* (Deuteronomy 31:20). We tend to cling to the Lord when it's obvious that He must provide our needs. After people become prosperous, they often take the Lord for granted, because they no longer think they have as much need of Him. Paul warned Timothy, *"Instruct those who are rich in this present world not . . . to fix their hope on the uncertainty of riches, but on God"* (1 Timothy 6:17).

Third, it is difficult for the rich to come to know Jesus Christ as their Savior. *"Jesus said to His disciples, 'Truly I say to you, it is hard for a rich man to enter the kingdom of heaven'"* (Matthew 19:23). Again, this is because the rich generally feel less of a need for God. Riches also can destroy a spiritually fruitful life. *"The one on whom seed was sown among the thorns, this is the man who hears the word, and the worry of the world and the deceitfulness of wealth choke the word, and it becomes unfruitful"* (Matthew 13:22). Riches are deceitful because they are tangible and can blind us from the reality of the unseen Lord. They seem to be able to do things that only Christ can really do.

WHY DO THE WICKED PROSPER?

This is a question God's people have asked for centuries. The prophet Jeremiah inquired of the Lord: *"You are always righteous, O Lord. . . . Yet I would speak with you about your justice: Why does the way of the wicked prosper?"* (Jeremiah 12:1, NIV).

> *Riches are deceitful because they are tangible and can blind us from the reality of the unseen Lord. They seem to be able to do things that only Christ can really do.*

The Psalmist also asked why the wicked prospered, because godliness did not seem to "pay off." Then the Lord revealed the wicked person's end—sudden eternal punishment:

> "Surely God is good to . . . those who are pure in heart. But as for me, my feet had almost slipped . . . for I envied the arrogant when I saw the prosperity of the wicked . . . When I tried to understand all this, it was oppressive to me till I entered the sanctuary of God; then I understood their final destiny. Surely you place them on slippery ground; you cast them down to ruin. How suddenly are they destroyed, completely swept away by terrors!" (Psalm 73:1-3, 16-19, NIV).

The Bible tells us that some of the wicked will prosper and not to envy them, because life on earth is short. *"Do not fret because of evil men or be envious of those who do wrong; for like the grass they will soon wither, like green plants they will soon die"* (Psalm 37:1-2, NIV). We are to maintain the Lord's perspective and His eternal value system.

LITIGATION

Thousands of lawsuits are filed each day in our country. Unfortunately, many of these pit Christian against Christian. Suing seems to be a national pastime. A woman sued a man who she said had kicked her at a nightclub. She sought $200,000 as compensation for the injury and lost time on the dance floor.

There are a number of reasons for this flood of lawsuits, including an avalanche of new laws and, most disturbing, that people are becoming less and less forgiving. The court system uses an adversarial process, which frequently creates animosities between the parties involved. Instead of trying to heal, the system provides a legal solution but leaves the problems of unforgiveness and anger untouched.

The Bible stresses that the goal should be reconciliation. *"If you are presenting your offering at the altar, and there remember that your brother has something against you, leave your offering there before the altar and go; first be reconciled to your brother"* (Matthew 5:23-24).

Scripture states that when Christians are at odds with one another they should not settle their disputes through the courts. *"Does any one of you, when he has a case against his neighbor, dare to go to law before the unrighteous and not before the saints? Or do you not know that the saints will judge the world? If the world is judged by you, are you not competent to constitute the smallest law courts? Do you not know that we shall judge angels? How much more matters of this life? So if you have law courts dealing with matters of this life, do you appoint them as judges who are of no account in the church? I say this to your shame. Is it so, that there is not among you one wise man who will be able to decide between his brethren, but brother goes to law with brother, and that before unbelievers? Actually, then, it is already a defeat for you, that you have lawsuits with one another. Why not rather be wronged? Why not rather be defrauded?"* (1 Corinthians 6:1-7).

Instead of initiating a lawsuit, a three-step procedure for Christians to resolve their differences is set forth in Matthew 18:15-17.

Instead of initiating a lawsuit, a three-step procedure for Christians to resolve their differences is set forth in Matthew 18:15-17: *"If your brother sins, go and show him his fault in private; if he listens to you, you have won your brother. But if he does not listen to you, take one or two more with you, so that by the mouth of two or three witnesses every fact may be confirmed. And if he refuses to listen to them, tell it to the church; and if he refuses to listen even to the church, let him be to you as a Gentile and a tax-collector."*

1. **Go in private.** The party who believes he or she has been wronged needs to confront the other person in private with his or her claims. If the dispute remains unresolved,
2. **Go with one or two others.** The person who feels wronged should return with witnesses who can confirm facts or help resolve the dispute. If this is still unsuccessful,
3. **Go before the church.** The third step is mediation or arbitration before an impartial group in the church or perhaps a conciliation service sponsored by a church or ministry, if this is available in your area.

The greatest benefit of following this procedure is not simply reaching a fair settlement of the dispute but practicing forgiveness and demonstrating love.

TAXES

What does the Bible say about paying taxes? That is the same question that was asked of Jesus. *"Is it lawful for us to pay taxes to Caesar, or not? . . .* [Jesus] *said to them, 'Show Me a denarius* [Roman coin]. *Whose likeness and inscription does it have?' They said, 'Caesar's.' And He said to them, 'Then give to Caesar the things that are Caesar's'"* (Luke 20:22-25). This is an example of the contrast between the practices of our society and the teaching of Scripture. Avoid paying taxes at any cost, people rationalize; after all, the government wastes much of what it collects.

"Oh great, now I have to give unto Caesar, too."

But the Bible tells us to pay our taxes: *"Every person is to be in subjection to the governing authorities. For there is no authority except from God, and those which exist are established by God. . . . Because of this you also pay taxes, for rulers are servants of God, devoting themselves to this very thing. Render to all what is due them: tax to whom tax is due"* (Romans 13:1, 6-7). It is permissible to reduce taxes by using legal tax deductions, but we should be careful not to make unwise decisions simply to avoid paying taxes.

Study carefully this passage.

> *"Do not hold your faith in our glorious Lord Jesus Christ with an attitude of personal favoritism. For if a man comes into your assembly with a gold ring and dressed in fine clothes, and there also comes in a poor man in dirty clothes, and you pay special attention to the one who is wearing the fine clothes . . . have you not made distinctions among yourselves, and become judges with evil motives? . . . If, however, you are fulfilling the royal law according to the Scripture, 'You shall love your neighbor as yourself,' you are doing well. But if you show partiality, you are committing sin and are convicted by the law as transgressors"* (James 2:1-9).

I have struggled with the sin of partiality, and this has unintentionally influenced my actions. Once, when I hung up the phone, my wife said, "I know you were not talking to Ken; it must have been Ryan. You like Ken better, and it shows in your voice."

Partiality does not have to be based on a person's wealth. It can also be based on a person's education, social position, or spiritual status. James 2:9 could not be more blunt: *"If you show partiality, you are committing sin and are convicted by the law as transgressors."* How do we break the habit of partiality? Romans 12:10 tells us, *"Be devoted to one another in brotherly love; give preference to one another in honor."* And Philippians 2:3 reads, *"With humility of mind regard one another as more important than yourselves."* We need to ask the Lord to ingrain in our thinking the habit of elevating each person to be more important than ourselves. One practical way to overcome partiality is to concentrate on the abilities of each person. Everyone can do some things better than I can. This realization helps me appreciate all people.

TEACHING CHILDREN

In 1904 the country of Wales experienced a remarkable revival. Thousands of people were introduced to Christ, and the results were dramatic. Bars closed because of lack of business. Policemen exchanged their weapons for white gloves because crime disappeared. Wales was so evangelically minded that it sent missionaries all over the world.

One of those missionaries traveled to Argentina where on the streets he led a young boy to Christ. The boy's name was Luis Palau. He has since become known as the "Billy Graham of Latin America." Palau visited Wales to express his thankfulness for being led to Christ. What he discovered was astonishing. Less than one-half of one percent of the Welsh attended church. Divorce was at an all-time high, and crime was increasing.

As a result of this experience, Palau produced a film titled *God Has No Grandchildren*. The thrust of the film is that each generation is responsible for

We need to ask the Lord to ingrain in our thinking the habit of consciously elevating each person to be more important than ourselves.

PERSPECTIVE NOTES

passing on the faith to the next. In Wales, the impact of Christianity had all but disappeared.

Each generation is responsible for passing on the truths of Scripture, including God's financial principles, to its children. Proverbs 22:6 says, *"Train up a child in the way he should go, even when he is old he will not depart from it."*

Answer this question: When you left home, how well prepared were you to make financial decisions? Parents and teachers spend years preparing young people for occupations but generally less than a few hours teaching children the value and use of the money they will earn during their careers. To teach God's financial principles, three methods should be used: verbal communication, modeling, and practical experience.

VERBAL COMMUNICATION

The Lord charged the Israelites, *"These words, which I am commanding you today, shall be on your heart. You shall teach them diligently to your sons and shall talk of them when you sit in your house and when you walk by the way and when you lie down and when you rise up"* (Deuteronomy 6:6-7). We must verbally instruct children in the ways of the Lord, but children need more than verbal instruction; they also need a good example.

MODELING

Children soak up parental attitudes toward money like a sponge soaks up water. Parents need to be models of how to handle money wisely. Paul recognized the importance of example when he said, *"Be imitators of me, just as I also am of Christ"* (1 Corinthians 11:1).

Luke 6:40 is a challenging passage. It reads, *"Everyone, after he has been fully trained, will be like his teacher."* Another way of saying this is that we can teach what we believe, but we only reproduce who we are. We must be good models.

PRACTICAL EXPERIENCES

Children then need to be given opportunities to apply what they have heard and seen. There are learning experiences that benefit the child in the area of money management and money making.

LEARNING EXPERIENCES IN MONEY MANAGEMENT
Learning to handle money should be part of a child's education. This is a part which the parents must direct themselves and not delegate to teachers, because spending experiences are found outside the classroom. Consider five areas in which this is possible.

Each generation is responsible for passing on the gospel and truths of Scripture, including God's financial priniples, to its children.

1. Income

As soon as children are ready for school, they should begin to receive incomes to manage. Parents need to decide whether the children must earn the income or if they wish to give an allowance.

The amount of the income will vary according to as the child's age, the ability to earn, and the financial circumstances of the family. However, the amount of the income is not as important as the responsibility of handling money. At first it is a new experience, and the child will make many mistakes. Do not hesitate to let the "law of natural consequences" run its course. You are going to be tempted to help when the child spends all the income the first day on an unwise purchase. *But do not bail out the child!* Mistakes will be the best teacher.

Parents should establish boundaries and offer advice on how to spend money, but your child must have freedom of choice within those boundaries. The first few pennies will make a lasting impression.

Every Saturday I used to bicycle to the store with my son, Matthew, to buy him a pack of gum. Despite my advice, the entire pack would be consumed that day.

When he started to earn money, we decided that Matthew would have to buy his gum. I will never forget the pained expression on his face as he came out of the store with his first purchase. "This gum cost me all my money!" he moaned. That pack of gum lasted a week. Parents should slowly increase the allowance as the child grows in ability and demonstrates wise spending patterns.

2. Budgeting

When children start to receive an income, teach them how to budget. Begin with a simple system, using a three-compartment bank, each compartment labeled separately: give, save, and spend. The child distributes a portion of the income into each compartment. Thus a simple budget is established by using visual control. Even a six-year-old can understand this method, because when there is no more money to spend, the bank is empty!

As children mature, they should participate in the family budget to help them understand the limitations of the family income. When children become teenagers, they should begin a written budget. It is wise to train teens to use one of the budgeting software programs that are available. During the budget training, teach the child to become a wise consumer. Teach shopping skills, the ability to distinguish needs from wants, and the importance of waiting on the Lord to provide. Warn the child about the powerful influence of advertising and the danger of impulse spending.

3. Saving and Investing

The habit of saving should begin as soon as the child receives an income. It is helpful to open a savings account in the child's name. As children mature, expose them to various types of investments: stocks, bonds, and so forth. Also, teach children the benefits of compounding interest. If they grasp this con-

The giving-saving-spending bank has been designed to teach your child how to handle money in a way that is pleasing to God. Contact us to order.

cept and become faithful savers, they will enjoy financial stability as adults. Parents should demonstrate this by saving for something that will directly benefit the children. Use a graph the children can fill in so they can visually chart the progress of saving.

Children should have both short-term and long-term saving goals. The younger the child, the more important short-term goals are. To four-year-olds, a week seems like a lifetime to save for a purchase. They will not understand saving for their future education but will get excited about saving for a small toy.

4. Debt

Also teach how difficult it is to get out of debt. A father loaned his son and daughter money to buy bicycles. He drew up a credit agreement with a schedule for repayment of the loan. After they went through the long process of paying off the loan, the family celebrated with a "mortgage burning" ceremony. The children appreciated those bikes more than any of their other possessions and decided to avoid debt in the future.

5. Giving

The best time to establish the habit of giving is when a child is young. It is helpful for children to give a portion of their gifts to a need they can see. For example, children understand when their gifts help build the church or buy food for a needy family they know.

Richard Halverson, former U. S. Senate chaplain, gave his son, Chris, this heritage as a child. Chris gave money to support Kim, an orphan who had lost his sight during the Korean War. Chris was taught to feel that Kim was like an adopted brother. One Christmas, Chris bought Kim a harmonica. Kim cherished this gift from Chris and learned to play it well. Today, Kim is an evangelist, and his presentation of the Gospel includes playing the harmonica.

When your child is a teenager, serving at a local homeless shelter or taking a mission trip to a country where there is deep poverty can be a powerful experience. Exposure to poverty can initiate a lifetime of giving to the poor. We also recommend a family time each week for dedicating that week's gifts to the Lord.

LEARNING EXPERIENCES IN MONEY MAKING

Parents also have the responsibility to train children to develop proper work habits. If the children learn how to work with the proper attitude, they will become valuable commodities in the job market. Good employees are difficult to find. There are four areas to consider in this training.

1. Learning Routine Responsibilities

The best way for a child to become faithful in work is to establish the habit of daily household chores. These are chores that each member of the family is expected to perform.

2. Expose Your Children to Your Work

Many children do not know how their fathers or mothers earn income. An important way to teach the value of work is to expose children to the parents' means of making a living.

One word of advice: Because most children are not with their parents at work, parents' work habits around the home will be a major influence. If a parent works hard away from home but complains about washing the dishes at home, what is being communicated to the children about work? Examine your work activities at home to ensure that you are properly influencing your children.

3. Working for Others

Baby-sitting, bagging groceries, or waiting on tables will be an education. A job gives a child an opportunity to enter into an employee-employer relationship and to earn extra money. The objective of teaching children the value of work is to build character. A working child with the proper attitude will be a more satisfied individual. He or she will grow up with more respect for the value of money and the effort required to earn it.

4. Career Direct—YES!®

The Career Direct—Youth Exploration Survey® helps point students ages 13-16 toward a fulfilling future career. It covers four areas: personality, vocational interests, abilities, and priorities. It is designed to be fun, informative, and interactive. It is biblically based and can be used for an individual or a group. To order, contact CROWN.

PRAYER

One of the more valuable lessons you can teach children is to seek the Lord's guidance and provision through prayer. The Lord wants to demonstrate that He is actively involved in our lives. One way He does this is by answering our prayers. We often rob ourselves of this opportunity by buying things or charging purchases without praying for the Lord to supply them.

One couple decided to ask their son to pray for some shirts he needed. After several months, a friend in the clothing business called to ask if their son needed shirts because he had excess inventory in his size. They excitedly responded, "Absolutely!" Their friend brought 10 shirts to their home! That evening as their son began to pray for his shirts, the father said, "You no longer need to pray for those shirts. God has answered your prayers." They brought out the shirts one-by-one. By the tenth shirt, their son thought God was in the shirt business.

Single Parents

Single parents are increasingly common, and if you are one, we appreciate the added demands you face. Be encouraged—God defends the cause of single-parent families: *"He executes justice for the orphan and the widow, and shows His love . . . by giving him food and clothing"* (Deuteronomy 10:18). And He sustains the fatherless: *"The Lord . . . supports the fatherless and the widow"* (Psalm 146:9).

Grandparents

If you are a grandparent, you have a special opportunity to influence your grandchildren. We recommend that parents meet with grandparents and design together a strategy for training the grandchildren how to handle money. It is important for grandparents to play a role in which they complement the objectives of the parents. Too often parents and grandparents have not reached an agreement on how to train the next generation. This can lead to bruised relationships and ineffective training.

STRATEGY FOR INDEPENDENCE

Finally, it is wise to establish a strategy for independence. Lyle and Marge Nelsen have four mature and responsible children. They had their children manage all of their own finances (with the exception of food and shelter) by the senior year in high school. In this way they could be available to advise the children as they learned to make spending decisions.

As the people of Wales discovered, God has no grandchildren. Passing our faith in Christ to the next generation can be compared to a relay race. Any track coach will tell you relay races can be won or lost in the passing of the baton from one runner to another. Seldom is the baton dropped once it is firmly in the grasp of a runner. If it is going to be dropped, it is in the exchange between the runners. Adults have the responsibility to pass the baton of practical biblical truths to the younger generation. At times during the training it may seem as if there is little progress. But be *consistent and persistent!* May our generation leave our children the blessed legacy of financial faithfulness.

To help parents and teachers train children to handle money God's way, CROWN FINANCIAL MINISTRIES has developed four outstanding studies. The three studies for younger children may be taught in a variety of settings—one-on-one, in small groups, and in a classroom. No special teacher training is required for these studies.

The **ABCs of Handling Money God's Way** (for children ages 7 and younger) and **The Secret** (for children 8 to 12) are fully illustrated storybooks that make learning basic financial principles fun and exciting! The *Leader's Guide* for each book provides a wide variety of activities that reinforce these principles.

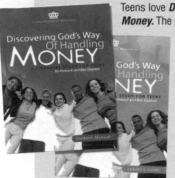

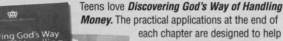

Teens love **Discovering God's Way of Handling Money.** The practical applications at the end of each chapter are designed to help teens begin habits that will set them on a lifelong journey of handling money God's way.

CROWN'S **Collegiate Edition** is an excellent study to teach God's perspective of money at this formative time of their lives. It may be taught in a small group or college classroom.

CROWN FINANCIAL MINISTRIES
PO Box 100
Gainesville GA 30503-0100
1-800-722-1976
Crown.org

PERSPECTIVE NOTES

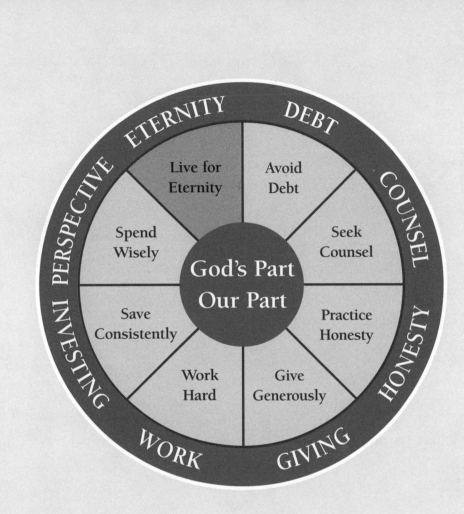

All Will Give an Account

*"What does it profit a man to gain the
whole world, and forfeit his soul?"*
(Mark 8:36).

ETERNITY HOMEWORK

Scripture to Memorize

"What does it profit a man to gain the whole world, and forfeit his soul?"
(Mark 8:36).

Practical Application: ☐ Complete the Financial Goals practical application. ☐ Also complete and return the Involvement and Suggestions sheet found in the back of the *Practical Application Workbook*.

DAY ONE

Read the Perspective Notes on pages 141 to 156.

1. What was the most helpful concept you learned from the notes?

2. Do you sense the Lord would have you alter your lifestyle in any way? If so, in what way?

DAY TWO

Read *Psalm 39:4-6* and *Psalm 103:13-16*.

1. What do these passages say to you about the length of life on earth?

ETERNITY

Read *Psalm 90:10, 12.*

2. Why do you think that Moses suggested numbering your days?

3. Estimate the number of days you have left on earth. How does this impact your thinking?

4. Based on your number of days, what actions will you take?

DAY THREE

Read *1 Chronicles 29:15; Philippians 3:20; and 1 Peter 2:11.*

1. What do these passages say about your identity on earth and in heaven?

   1 Chronicles 29:15—

   Philippians 3:20—

   1 Peter 2:11—

Read *2 Peter 3:10-13.*

2. In the future, what will happen to the earth?

3. How should this impact the way you invest your time and spend money?

Read *Ecclesiates 12:13-14* **and** *2 Corinthians 5:9-10.*

1. What will happen to each of us in the future?

    Ecclesiates 12:13-14—

    2 Corinthians 5:9-10—

Read *1 Corinthians 3:11-15.*

2. How would you describe the works (give some examples) that will be burned at this final judgment?

3. Give some examples of works that will be rewarded.

4. What are you doing that will survive this final judgment?

Read *2 Corinthians 4:18*.

1. What does this verse say to you?

2. As you reflect on eternity, answer thoughtfully: What three things do I want to accomplish during the rest of my life?

3. What can I do during my lifetime that would contribute most significantly to the cause of Christ?

4. In light of these answers, what actions or changes do I need to make?

DAY SIX

Read the Eternity notes on pages 163 to 170.

1. What was the most important concept you learned from reading the notes?

2. Be sure you have completed the Involvement and Suggestions sheet on page 109 in the *Practical Application Workbook*. Your opinion is important to us—so important that we have chosen to present a thank you gift to everyone who will take the few minutes necessary to fill out and return the sheet. Please fold and seal the completed sheet and drop it in the mail. Postage is prepaid. Or, if you prefer to complete the sheet online, go to **www.crown.org/isform.asp**. Please take a moment to complete the sheet *today*.

3. Describe what has been the most beneficial part of the Small Group Study for you.

 Please write your prayer requests in your Prayer Log before coming to class.

 I will take the following action as a result of this week's study.

ETERNITY NOTES

Please do not read these notes until you have completed the Eternity Homework.

On Monday, October 25, 1999, an unusual story was reported on the news. A private jet originating from Orlando, Florida was followed by Air Force jets that were unable to communicate with the pilots. Later I learned that two close friends of mine, Robert Fraley and Van Ardan, were on the airplane that carried golfer Payne Stewart to his death.

One of the most critical principles for us to understand is the reality of eternity. Robert and Van were men in their mid-forties. One of their most distinctive characteristics was that they lived with an eternal perspective. Robert had framed these words in his workout area, "Take care of your body as though you will live forever; take care of your soul as if you will die tomorrow."

Because God loves us, He reveals in the Scriptures that there is a heaven and hell, that there is a coming judgment, and that He will grant eternal rewards unequally. The Lord wants the very best for us. Therefore, He wants to motivate us to invest our lives in such a way that we can enjoy an intimate relationship with Him now and receive the greatest possible rewards and responsibilities in heaven.

Our failure to view our present lives through the lens of eternity is one of the biggest hindrances to seeing our lives and our assets in their true light. Yet Scripture states that the reality of our eternal future should determine the character of our present lives and the use of our money and possessions.

People who do not know the Lord look at life as a brief interval that begins at birth and ends at death. Looking to the future they see no further than their own life span. With no eternal perspective, they think, *If this life is all there is, why deny myself any pleasure or possession?*

Those who know Christ are people of an entirely different perspective. We know life is short; it is the preface—not the book, the preliminaries—not the main event. It is the testing period that will determine much of our experience in heaven.

Financial planners have a hard time convincing people to look down the road, instead of simply focusing on today. "Don't think this year," they will tell you. "Think 30 years from now by planning." The wise person does indeed think ahead, but far more than 30 years—30 million years ahead. As someone once said, "He who provides for this life but takes no care for eternity is wise for a moment but a fool forever." Jesus said it this way, *"What does it profit a man to gain the whole world, and forfeit his soul?"* (Mark 8:36).

> *The reality of our eternal future should determine the character of our present life and the use of our money and possessions.*

Throughout the Bible we are reminded that life on earth is brief: "[God] *is mindful that we are but dust*" (Psalm 103:14). Our earthly bodies are called "*tents*" (2 Peter 1:13, NIV), temporary dwelling places of our eternal souls. David recognized this and sought to gain God's perspective in light of the brevity of life. He asked of the Lord, "*Show me, O Lord, my life's end and the number of my days; let me know how fleeting is my life. . . . Each man's life is but a breath. Man is a mere phantom as he goes to and fro: He bustles about, but only in vain; he heaps up wealth, not knowing who will get it*" (Psalm 39:4-6, NIV).

When a good friend discovered she had only a short time to live, she told me of her radical change in perspective. "The most striking thing that's happened," she said, "is that I find myself almost totally uninterested in accumulating more things. Things used to matter to me, but now I find my thoughts are centered on Christ, my friends, and other people."

Moses realized that true wisdom flowed out of understanding that our lives are short. So he asked the Lord to help him number the days he had on earth.

> "*As for the days of our life, they contain seventy years, or if due to strength, eighty years . . . for soon it is gone and we fly away. . . . So teach us to number our days, that we may present to You a heart of wisdom*" (Psalm 90:10,12).

I encourage you to number the days you estimate that you have left on earth. If I live as long as my father, I have about 9,000 days left. This has helped me become aware that I need to invest my life and resources in eternally important matters.

When I served in the Navy, my attention was focused on the town in which I was stationed. However, as soon as I received orders discharging me in two months, I became what was called a "short-timer." My focus then completely shifted from the town I was going to leave to my hometown. In a similar way, when we realize that we are really "short-timers" on earth, and that soon we will be going to our real home, our focus will shift to things that will be important in heaven. In light of the brevity of life, author Matthew Henry said, "It ought to be the business of every day to prepare for our last day."

Eternity Is Long

Eternity, on the other hand, *never ends*. It is forever. Imagine a cable running through the room where you are now. The cable runs out of the room to your right millions of light years all the way to the end of the universe and to your left to the other end of the universe. Now imagine that the cable to your left represents eternity past, and the cable to your right eternity future. You place a small mark on the cable in front of you. The mark represents your brief life on earth.

Because most people do not have an eternal perspective, they live as if the mark is all there is. They make mark choices; they live in mark houses, drive mark cars, wear mark clothes, live mark lifestyles, and raise mark children.

Devotional writer A.W. Tozer referred to eternity as the "the long tomorrow." This is the backdrop against which all the questions of life and the handling of our resources must be answered.

ALIENS AND PILGRIMS

Scripture tells us several things about our identity and role on this earth. First of all, *"Our citizenship is in heaven"* (Philippians 3:20), not earth. Second, *"We are ambassadors for Christ"* (2 Corinthians 5:20) representing Him on earth. Imagine yourself an ambassador from a country who goes to work in another country that is generally hostile to your own. Naturally, you will want to learn about this new place, see the sights, and become familiar with the people and culture. But suppose eventually you become so much part of this foreign country that you begin to regard it as your true home. Your allegiance wavers, and you gradually compromise your position as an ambassador, becoming increasingly ineffective in representing the best interests of your own country.

We must never become too much at home in this world or we will become ineffective in serving the cause of the kingdom we are here to represent. We are aliens, strangers, and pilgrims on earth. Peter wrote, *"Live your lives as strangers here in reverent fear"* (1 Peter 1:17, NIV). Later he added, *"I urge you, as aliens and strangers in the world, to abstain from sinful desires"* (1 Peter 2:11, NIV). Another Bible translation uses the words *"strangers and pilgrims"* (KJV).

Pilgrims are unattached. They are travelers—not settlers—aware that the excessive accumulation of things can distract. Material things are valuable to pilgrims, but only as they facilitate their mission. Things can entrench us in the present world. They can be like chains around our legs, making us unresponsive to God. If our eyes are focused on the visible, they will be drawn away from the invisible. *"So we fix our eyes not on what is seen, but on what is unseen. For what is seen is temporary, but what is unseen is eternal"* (2 Corinthians 4:18, NIV).

Pilgrims of faith look to the next world. They see earthly possessions for what they are: useful for kingdom purposes but far too flimsy to bear the weight of trust. Thomas à Kempis, author of *The Imitation of Christ*, said it this way, "Let temporal things serve your use, but the eternal be the object of your desire." There are two principles concerning our possessions that will help us gain a proper perspective of them.

1. We Leave It All Behind

After wealthy John D. Rockefeller died, his accountant was asked how much he left. The accountant responded, "He left it all." Job said it this way, *"Naked I came from my mother's womb, and naked I shall return there"* (Job 1:21). Paul wrote, *"We have brought nothing into the world, so we cannot take anything out of it either"* (1 Timothy 6:7).

The psalmist observed, *"Do not be afraid when a man becomes rich, when the glory of his house is increased; for when he dies he will carry nothing away;*

> *"Let temporal things serve your use, but the eternal be the object of your desire."*
> —THOMAS À KEMPIS

his glory will not descend after him. Though while he lives he congratulates himself—and though men praise you when you do well for yourself—he shall go to the generation of his fathers" (Psalm 49:16-20).

2. Everything Will Be Destroyed

Earthly goods will not last forever—they are destined to be totally annihilated. *"The day of the Lord will come like a thief. The heavens will disappear with a roar; the elements will be destroyed by fire, and the earth and everything in it will be laid bare. Since everything will be destroyed in this way, what kind of people ought you to be? You ought to live holy and godly lives"* (2 Peter 3:10-11, NIV). Understanding the temporary nature of possessions should influence us as we consider spending decisions.

JUDGMENT

It is uncomfortable to think about judgment. But because our Lord loves us so deeply, He wanted us to realize what would happen in the future. Therefore, God revealed to us that everyone will be judged according to our deeds: *"He has fixed a day in which He will judge the world in righteousness"* (Acts 17:31). All of us should live each day with this awareness: *"They will have to give an account to Him who is ready to judge the living and the dead"* (1 Peter 4:5, NIV).

God will judge us with total knowledge: *"Nothing in all creation is hidden from God's sight. Everything is uncovered and laid bare before the eyes of Him to whom we must give account"* (Hebrews 4:13, NIV). Because His knowledge is total, his judgment is comprehensive: *"Men will have to give account on the day of judgment for every careless word they have spoken"* (Matthew 12:36, NIV). His judgment extends to what is hidden from people. *"God will bring every deed into judgment, including every hidden thing, whether it is good or evil"* (Ecclesiastes 12:14, NIV). He will even *"disclose the motives of men's hearts"* (1 Corinthians 4:5).

The Bible teaches that all those who do not know Christ will be judged at the Great White Throne and sent to an indescribably dreadful place.

> *"I saw a great white throne and Him who was seated on it . . . and I saw the dead, great and small, standing before the throne. . . . Each person was judged according to what he had done. . . . If anyone's name was not found written in the book of life, he was thrown into the lake of fire"* (Revelation 20:11-15, NIV).

Judgment of Believers

After they die, those who know Christ will spend eternity with the Lord in Heaven, an incredibly wonderful place. But what we seldom consider is that the entry point to heaven is a judgment.

Scripture teaches that all believers in Christ will give an account of their lives to the Lord. *"We shall all stand before the judgment seat of God. . . . So then each of us will give an account of himself to God"* (Romans 14:10,12). The result of this will be the gain or loss of eternal rewards. In 1 Corinthians 3:13-15 (NIV) it reads, *"His work will be shown for what it is, because the* [Judgment]

Day will bring it to light. . . . If what he has built survives, he will receive his reward. If it is burned up, he will suffer loss." Our works are what we have done with our time, influence, talents, and resources. God's Word does not treat this judgment as just a meaningless formality before we get on to the real business of heaven. Rather, Scripture presents it as a monumental event in which things of eternal significance are brought to light.

MOTIVATION AND REWARDS

Why should I follow Scripture's guidance on money and possessions when it is so much fun to do whatever I please with my resources? I'm a Christian. I know I'm going to heaven anyway. Why not have the best of both worlds—this one and the next? Though few of us would be honest enough to use such language, these questions reflect a common attitude.

The prospect of eternal rewards for our obedience is a neglected key to unlocking our motivation. Paul was motivated by the prospect of eternal rewards. He wrote, *"I have fought the good fight, I have finished the course, I have kept the faith; in the future there is laid up for me the crown of righteousness, which the Lord, the righteous Judge, will award to me on that day"* (2 Timothy 4:7-8). The Lord appeals not only to our compassion but also to our eternal self-interest. *"Love your enemies, and do good, and lend, expecting nothing in return; and your reward will be great"* (Luke 6:35).

Our heavenly Father uses three things to motivate us to obey Him: the love of God, the fear of God, and the rewards of God. These are the same motivations that move my children to obey me. My children love me, and sometimes this is sufficient for them to be obedient. But other times it isn't enough. In a healthy sense, they also fear me. They know I will discipline them for wrongdoings. They also know I will reward them for doing right, with my words of approval and sometimes in tangible ways.

Unequal Rewards in Heaven
It is not as simple as saying, "I'll be in heaven and that's all that matters." On the contrary, Paul spoke about the loss of reward as a terrible loss. The receiving of rewards from Christ is an unspeakable gain. Not all Christians will have the same rewards in heaven.

John Wesley said, "I value all things only by the price they shall gain in eternity." God's kingdom was the reference point for him. He lived as he did, not because he didn't treasure things but because he treasured the right things. We often miss something in missionary martyr Jim Elliott's famous words, "He is no fool who gives what he cannot keep to gain what he cannot lose." We focus on Elliott's willingness to sacrifice, and so we should; however, we often overlook his motivation for gain. What separated him from many Christians was not that he did not want treasure but that he wanted *real* treasure. Remember God loves you deeply. Because He wants the best for you throughout eternity, God has revealed that today's sacrifices and service for Him will pay off forever.

John Wesley said, "I value all things only by the price they shall gain in eternity."

Our daily choices will determine what will happen in the future. What we do in this life is of eternal importance. We only live on this earth once. *"It is appointed for men to die once and after this comes judgment"* (Hebrews 9:27). There is no such thing as reincarnation. Once our life on earth is over, we will never have another chance to move the hand of God through prayer, to share Christ with one who does not know the Savior, to give money to further God's kingdom, or to share with the needy.

Those who dabble in photography understand the effect of the "fixer." In developing a photograph, the negatives are immersed in several different solutions. The developing solution parallels this life. As long as the photograph is in the developer solution it is subject to change. But when it is dropped in the fixer or "stop bath," it is permanently fixed. The photograph is then done. So it will be when we enter eternity: the lives we live on earth will be fixed as is, never to be altered or revised.

Alfred Nobel was a Swedish chemist who made a fortune by inventing dynamite and explosives for weapons. When Nobel's brother died, a newspaper accidentally printed Alfred's obituary instead. He was described as a man who became rich by enabling people to kill each other with powerful weapons. Shaken from this assessment, Nobel resolved to use his fortune to reward accomplishments that benefited humanity, including what we now know as the Nobel Peace Prize. Let us put ourselves in Nobel's place. Let us read our own obituary, not as written by people but as it would be written from heaven's point of view. Then let us use the rest of our lives to edit that obituary into what we really want it to be.

When I was a young boy I used to love playing Little League baseball. We played on a huge baseball field that had towering fences in the outfield. Years later, shortly after my father died, I spent the day walking around my old hometown reflecting on his life. When I visited the baseball field, I was shocked! It was so small. You could actually step over the outfield fences. While standing on the pitcher's mound a thought struck me: Many of those things that seem so large and important to us today shrink to insignificance in just a few years.

When I am face to face with Christ and look back on my life, I want to see that the things in which I invested my time, creativity, influence, and assets are big things to the Lord. I do not want to squander my life on things that will not matter throughout eternity.

When Moses lived, Pharaoh was the most powerful person on earth. Pharaoh's daughter adopted Moses as an infant, and he had the opportunity to enjoy the wealth and prestige of a member of the royal family. Hebrews 11:24-26 tells us what Moses later chose and why he decided it. *"By faith Moses, when he had grown up, refused to be called the son of Pharaoh's daughter, choosing rather to endure ill-treatment with the people of God than to enjoy the passing pleasures of sin, considering the reproach of Christ greater riches than the treasures of Egypt; for he was looking to the reward."* Because Moses was looking forward to the only real rewards that

Our daily choices will determine what will happen in the future. What we do in this life is of eternal importance.

ETERNITY NOTES

would last, he chose to become a Hebrew slave and was used by God in a remarkable way.

What are the choices facing you now? How does an eternal perspective influence your decisions? Martin Luther said that on his calendar there were only two days: "today" and "that Day." May we invest all that we are and have today in light of *that* day.

GOING DEEPER

Author **Randy C. Alcorn** graciously contributed much of this chapter from his outstanding book *Money, Possessions and Eternity*. (Used by permission of Tyndale House Publishers, Inc. All rights reserved.) We heartily recommend it to you.

LET'S REVIEW

At the beginning of this study we asked why the Bible said so much about money—in more than 2,350 verses. There are three major spiritual reasons: how we handle money impacts our fellowship with the Lord, money is the primary competitor with Christ for the lordship of our life, and money molds our characters. Another reason is that the Lord wants us to have a blueprint, a road map, for handling money so that we can become financially faithful in very practical ways.

Review this diagram of the wheel again. The eight areas of our responsibilities, each with its primary thrust, are identified.

Faithfulness Is a Journey
Applying the financial principles of Scripture is a journey that takes time. It's easy to become discouraged when your finances aren't completely under control by the end of this study. It takes the average person at least a year to apply most of these principles. Many CROWN graduates decide to lead the study because they know the leaders learn more than anyone else. As they help their students, the leaders make progress on their own financial journey.

Faithfulness in Small Matters Is Foundational
Some people also become frustrated by the inability to solve their financial problems quickly. Remember, simply be faithful with what you have—whether it is little or much. Some abandon the goal of becoming debt free or increasing their saving or giving, because the task looks impossible. And it may be— without the Lord's help. Your job is to make a genuine effort, no matter how small it may appear and then leave the results to God. I love what the Lord said to the prophet Zechariah, *"For who has despised the day of small things?"* (Zechariah 4:10). Don't be discouraged. Be diligent. Be persistent. Be faithful in even the smallest matters. Repeatedly we've seen the Lord bless those who tried to be faithful.

We are not economists. However, it is probable that our country will experience financially difficult times in the future. We don't know when this will occur or how it will manifest itself. We believe God has graciously given us a window of time to conform to His Word in the area of money. We plead with you to seize this opportunity! Become diligent in your efforts to get out of debt, give generously, budget, and work as unto the Lord. In short, become a faithful steward.

You now know the biblical framework for managing money. But knowing is only half of the solution. You must act upon that knowledge. Jesus said, *"Everyone who hears these words of Mine and acts on them, may be compared to a wise man who built his house upon the rock. And the rain fell, and the floods came, and the winds blew and slammed against that house; and yet it did not fall, for it had been founded on the rock. Everyone who hears these words of Mine and does not act on them, will be like a foolish man who built his house on the sand. The rain fell, and the floods came, and the winds blew and slammed against that house; and it fell, and great was its fall"* (Matthew 7:24-27).

The economic rain, floods, and winds will someday come against this country's financial house. If you have acted and built your house upon the rock-solid principles found in Scripture, your house will not fall. One of the best ways to demonstrate your love for your family and friends is to get your financial house in order and encourage others to do the same.

If you have a desire to help others learn God's way of handling money, there are four places you can serve with CROWN as illustrated in the baseball diamond. First, you may serve individuals as a small group leader or budget counselor. They are the heroes of CROWN FINANCIAL MINISTRIES, because it is in the small group or one-on-one where life-changes take place. Second base represents the opportunity to serve as the church coordinator or on the church team, if you want to impact your entire church. If you have a desire to influence your community, third base is for those who serve on the city team. In order for CROWN to have a broad impact on a larger city, it is necessary to have a full-time city director and a team of volunteers. Home plate is for those who have a "missionary spirit" and wish to help introduce CROWN to other cities and even other countries.

Please tell your leader if you wish to become a leader or co-leader or if you choose to serve on the church team. If you want to serve your entire city or even beyond your city, contact CROWN FINANCIAL MINISTRIES at **www.crown.org**.

We appreciate the effort you have invested in this study. And we pray this has given you a greater appreciation for the Scriptures, helped you develop close friendships, and above all else nurtured your love for Jesus Christ. May the Lord richly bless you.

ETERNITY NOTES

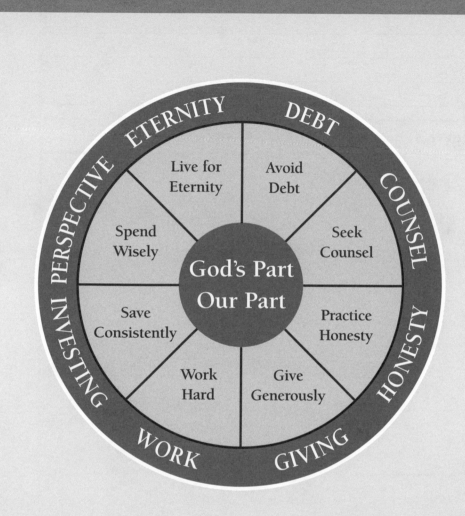

Be Faithful in Prayer

*"Pray for one another. . . . The effective prayer
of a righteous man can accomplish much"*
(James 5:16).

"Pray for one another" (James 5:16).

Name _____   Spouse _____

Home phone _____   Children (ages) _____

Business phone _____   _____

Cell phone _____   _____

E-mail _____   _____

Home address _____   _____

_____   _____

Week	Prayer Request(s)	Answers to Prayer
1		
2		
3		
4		
5		
6		
7		
8		
9		
10	My long-term prayer request:	

PRAYER LOG

"Pray for one another" (James 5:16).

Name _____   Spouse _____

Home phone _____   Children (ages) _____

Business phone _____   _____

Cell phone _____   _____

E-mail _____   _____

Home address _____   _____

_____   _____

Week	Prayer Request(s)	Answers to Prayer
1		
2		
3		
4		
5		
6		
7		
8		
9		
10	My long-term prayer request:	

PRAYER LOG

"Pray for one another" (JAMES 5:16).

Name _____   Spouse _____

Home phone _____   Children (ages) _____

Business phone _____   _____

Cell phone _____   _____

E-mail _____   _____

Home address _____   _____

_____   _____

WEEK	PRAYER REQUEST(S)	ANSWERS TO PRAYER
1		
2		
3		
4		
5		
6		
7		
8		
9		
10	My long-term prayer request:	

PRAYER LOG

"Pray for one another" (JAMES 5:16).

Name _____   Spouse _____

Home phone _____   Children (ages) _____

Business phone _____   _____

Cell phone _____   _____

E-mail _____   _____

Home address _____   _____

_____   _____

WEEK	PRAYER REQUEST(S)	ANSWERS TO PRAYER
1		
2		
3		
4		
5		
6		
7		
8		
9		
10	My long-term prayer request:	

PRAYER LOG

"Pray for one another" (JAMES 5:16).

Name _____   Spouse _____

Home phone _____   Children (ages) _____

Business phone _____   _____

Cell phone _____   _____

E-mail _____   _____

Home address _____   _____

_____   _____

WEEK	PRAYER REQUEST(S)	ANSWERS TO PRAYER
1		
2		
3		
4		
5		
6		
7		
8		
9		
10	My long-term prayer request:	

PRAYER LOG

"Pray for one another" (JAMES 5:16).

Name _____   Spouse _____

Home phone _____   Children (ages) _____

Business phone _____   _____

Cell phone _____   _____

E-mail _____   _____

Home address _____   _____

_____   _____

WEEK	PRAYER REQUEST(S)	ANSWERS TO PRAYER
1		
2		
3		
4		
5		
6		
7		
8		
9		
10	My long-term prayer request:	

"Pray for one another" (JAMES 5:16).

Name _____   Spouse _____

Home phone _____   Children (ages) _____

Business phone _____   _____

Cell phone _____   _____

E-mail _____   _____

Home address _____   _____

_____   _____

WEEK	PRAYER REQUEST(S)	ANSWERS TO PRAYER
1		
2		
3		
4		
5		
6		
7		
8		
9		
10	My long-term prayer request:	

PRAYER LOG

"Pray for one another" (JAMES 5:16).

Name _____ Spouse _____

Home phone _____ Children (ages) _____

Business phone _____ _____

Cell phone _____ _____

E-mail _____ _____

Home address _____ _____

_____ _____

WEEK	PRAYER REQUEST(S)	ANSWERS TO PRAYER
1		
2		
3		
4		
5		
6		
7		
8		
9		
10	My long-term prayer request:	

"Pray for one another" (JAMES 5:16).

Name _____ Spouse _____

Home phone _____ Children (ages) _____

Business phone _____ _____

Cell phone _____ _____

E-mail _____ _____

Home address _____ _____

_____ _____

WEEK	PRAYER REQUEST(S)	ANSWERS TO PRAYER
1		
2		
3		
4		
5		
6		
7		
8		
9		
10	My long-term prayer request:	

PRAYER LOG

"Pray for one another" (JAMES 5:16).

Name _____ Spouse _____

Home phone _____ Children (ages) _____

Business phone _____ _____

Cell phone _____ _____

E-mail _____ _____

Home address _____ _____

_____ _____

Week	Prayer Request(s)	Answers to Prayer
1		
2		
3		
4		
5		
6		
7		
8		
9		
10	My long-term prayer request:	

PRAYER LOG

"Pray for one another" (JAMES 5:16).

Name _____   Spouse _____

Home phone _____   Children (ages) _____

Business phone _____   _____

Cell phone _____   _____

E-mail _____   _____

Home address _____   _____

_____   _____

Week	Prayer Request(s)	Answers to Prayer
1		
2		
3		
4		
5		
6		
7		
8		
9		
10	My long-term prayer request:	

PRAYER LOG